Oracle APEX
- The Tailor Fit

Rajan Chandru
Sathya Jegan N
Pandimuneeswaran K
Karthik S

DOYENSYS

Technology Drives, We Lead

notionpress
.com

INDIA • SINGAPORE • MALAYSIA

Notion Press

Old No. 38, New No. 6
McNichols Road, Chetpet
Chennai - 600 031

First Published by Notion Press 2019
Copyright © Doyensys 2019
All Rights Reserved.

ISBN 978-1-64760-813-2

Contents

INTRODUCTION

Oracle Application Express, otherwise referred to as APEX and pronounced as ā'pĕks, is a web-based, low-code rapid application that can be scalable and more secure.

Oracle APEX is a no-cost feature of Oracle Databasethat can run on any Oracle Database, whether it is on-premise or cloud or anywhere else. There is no additional licensing fee for APEX and Oracle fully supports it.

Oracle APEX is native to Oracle Database; hence all features and capabilities of Oracle Database can be utilized to develop and deploy APEX based applications.

Oracle APEX accelerates the development of applications to a greatextent since APEX has many built-in features such as user interface themes, navigation controls, form handlers and reports.

Oracle APEX applications can be created using the inbuilt wizards for creating various components like pages, items, buttons etc. APEX is built using SQL and PL/SQL and hence the attributes or valuescaptured in each wizard will be saved and archived in Oracle tables.

In Oracle APEX, a visually appealing application can be developed swiftly using the feature of drag and drop of objects resulting in less coding. Hence an APEX developer need not be proficient for web development technologies; instead, a developer could focus on the business challenge rather upon coding.

Oracle APEX application is a collection of linked pages using tabs, buttons or hypertext links. APEX also has an interactive user interface (UI) that enables users to display information stored in the Oracle Database and optionally to add, update or delete data. This UI can presentdetailsin many formats which includes static and interactive reports, interactive grids, forms, charts and maps.

Oracle APEX based applications are highly responsive UI where the business users can customize interactive grids and interactive reports. With an interactive grid or report, business users can customize the appearance of report data through searching, filtering, sorting, column selection, highlighting and other data manipulations. Also, business users can save their customizations and download the report locally.

Oracle APEX based applications can be developed by a developer using SQL, PLSQL for server-side and HTML, CSS, JAVASCRIPT for the client-side requirements.Oracle APEX enables the developer to customize the inbuilt components based on the Business requirement. *We shall explore in this book, the inbuilt features of Oracle APEX and how-to Tailor- fit the features of Oracle APEX as per various business need.*

ARCHITECTURE

Oracle APEX uses 3-tier architecture. It consists of browser for client tier, Oracle APEX engine for data tier and the preferred Oracle REST Data Services (ORDS) running in a Java Server for mid-tier.

Mid-tier can also be any of the following: Oracle Web-Logic Server (WLS) or Tomcat or Oracle Glassfish or Oracle Embedded PL/SQL Gateway (EPG) which is part of the Oracle DB or Oracle HTTP Server (OHS) with mod_plsql. *From Oracle release 12.1.3, Oracle HTTP Server (OHS), the mod_plsql feature has been deprecated.*

Page requests and submissions from the browser pass through the mid-tier to execute in the Database are returned as HTML responses to the browser. Mid-tier does not perform any data manipulation or processing, instead the APEX engine (inside the Oracle DB) processes the page and interacts with the data schemas in the DB.

2.1 ORDS

ORDS is the abbreviation of Oracle Rest Data Service and it is a java program that allows user to interact with the oracle database via REST service. The SQL or PL/SQL calls from the browser is transmitted to the oracle database and the result set from the Oracle Database is sent back to the ORDS which transforms the output to JSON format which will be sent back to the browser.

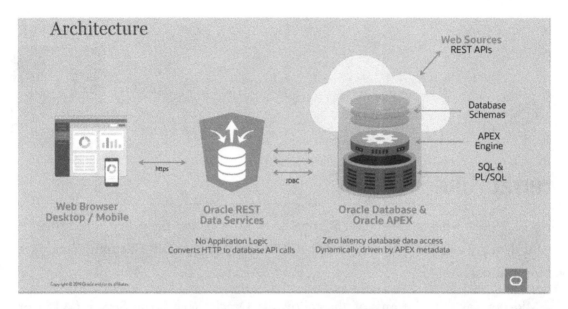

*Source: https://static.rainfocus.com/oracle/oow19/sess/1553127714132001Jbvx/PF/APEX_*
REST_DEV3246_1568745382889001IxQu.pdf

Oracle database 10g and 11g uses 2-tier architecture. It consists of browser for client tier, Oracle APEX engine for Data Tier. The APEX Engine renders HTML pages and processes page submissions based on the meta data within the DB. To establish communication between the browser and database, APEX Listener, Embedded PL/SQL Gateway (EPG) which is part of the Database or Apache and mod_plsql is configured.

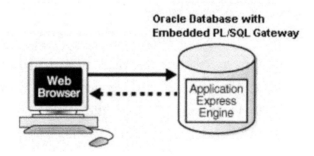

Source: https://docs.oracle.com/cd/E11882_01/appdev.112/e11947/start_arch.htm#
HTMDB25001

2.2 MULTITENANCY

Multitenancy is a software architecture in which single instances of software that run on a server and serves multiple tenants.

Oracle released Multitenant architecture from Database 12c Release 1 (12.1). In the Multitenant architecture, Oracle Database functions as a multitenant Container Database (CDB). A CDB comprises zero or more customer-created pluggable databases (PDBs). A PDB is a collection of schemas, schema objects and non-schema objects that can be plugged or unplugged from a CDB. All Oracle databases before Oracle Database 12*c* were non-CDBs. A PDB appears to an Oracle Net client as non-CDBs when it is actually managed within a CDB that may contain other PDBs.

2.3 APPLICATION CONTAINER

Application containers are a new feature in Oracle Database 12c Release 2 (12.2). Application containers are similar to a mini CDB. They contain metadata of the applications and common data across Application PDB's. For every application container, there is always one application root PDB that serves as a repository for a master definition of an application back end. An application root can house one or more applications, each made up of shared configuration, metadata and objects that are used by the pluggable databases associated with the application root.

Oracle APEX can be installed into an application container using the *apxappcon.sql* script. Multiple application containers can exist within a CDB,in which each container can have a different version of Oracle APEX.

An application container has the following containers:

- *Application root*: it can house one or more applications, each of them made up of shared configuration, metadata, code and objects that are used by the pluggable databases associated with it.
- *Application PDBs:* these are user created application plugged into the application root.

- *Application seed:* this is an optional application pluggable database tied up to application root which serves as a user-created template to create new applications.

2.3.1 Application Containers- Key Features

Application Master: A master application can be installed in one application root as an application container and it will be visible to all the application(s) pluggable databases in the application container.

Application Maintenance: As there is only one master copy of application the maintenance like patch applications can be performed only once at application root alone, the new definition will propagate to individual tenant pluggable databases after sync. And upgrade can be performed in a phased manner, leading to a much more agile application development process.

Application Versions: Different applications with distinct application names and application versions can be installed in an application container.

CHAPTER 3

ROADMAP OF **APEX**

Oracle APEX was developed way back in 2004, which was called HTML DB. Mike Hichwa, a developer at Oracle, created APEX, after the development of his previous project, Web DB, started to divaricate from his original vision. Before this release, it was released as Marvel. When tasked with building an internal web calendar, Hichwa enlisted the help of Joel Kallman and started development on a project called Flows. Hichwa and Kallman co-developed the Web Calendar and Flows, adding features to Flows as they needed them to develop the calendar. Early builds of Flow had no front-end, so all changes to an application had to be made in SQL*Plus via inserts, updates and deletes.

Source: https://www.youtube.com/watch?v=i_50UipxSEY; https://en.wikipedia.org/wiki/ Oracle_Application_Express

New features were added with each release of APEX. Oracle included new technology at each release, like in version 2, it was added with SQL workshop where it acts as GUI for executing query which has query builder as inbuilt for the ease of developers. Then they moved on in improving the user interface where they have built charts and reports. Later they have added migration guide and support for Oracle Forms to APEX which enable all the Oracle forms user to switch to the latest technology and helped them to speed up their development. In order to make the application feel lively, they havadded dynamic action and plugins which was handled by the developers using JavaScript. Inclusion of team development added advantage for the team to track the progress of the development.

The focus turned to mobile application as the world has shrunk to the individual's palm. Hence it's time for Oracle APEX to adapt itself for the same sothe responsive theme was added which will cater to this requirement of changing the display based on the screen resolution.

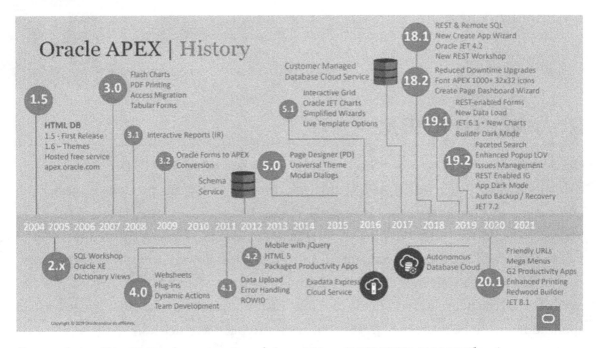

Source: https://static.rainfocus.com/oracle/oow19/sess/1553127714132001Jbvx/
PF/APEX_REST_DEV3246_1568745382889001IxQu.pdf

QUICK TOUR TO APEX

Each instance of the development of Oracle APEX may contain multiple workspaces. A workspace is a virtual, private database that permits many users to work inside an equivalent installation of Oracle APEX while keeping their objects, data and applications private.

Whenever you log in to Oracle APEX, the Workspace home page will appear with the main development components such as

- App Builder
- SQL workshop
- Team Development
- App Gallery

4.1 APP BUILDER

An application is a series of connected database-driven sites using tabs, buttons or hypertext links. The pages within the application shares a selected method of session state

9

and authentication. Application Builder is a method that you use to create the pages that form an app.

The App Builder home page displays all the installed applications in the current instance. The developers can select the edit button of the application to run, edit, import, export, copy or remove the application.

The App builder is further classified into create, import, dashboard and Workspace utilities as shown in the below screenshot.

Create   Import   Dashboard   Workspace Utilities

4.1.1 Create

Drives to .the Create Application Wizard where we can build the application from scratch or using spreadsheet or Packaged App (Productivity App) which comes along with Oracle APEX.

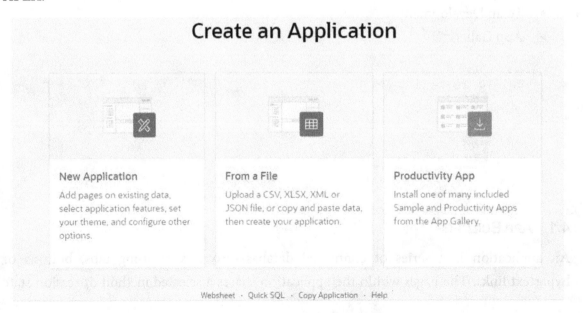

10

4.1.2 Import

Drives to the Import Wizard where we can-do import-export files from the export repository. This option is enabled for the file types like Database Application, Page or Component, Web sheet Application, Plug-in, Theme, UI Defaults and Team Development Feedbacks.

4.1.3 Dashboard

Nothing but just shows metrics about installed applications in the current workspace.

4.1.4 Workspace Utilities

Drives to the Workspace Utilities page where we can manage App Builder Defaults, REST Enabled SQL services, Remote Servers, Application Groups, Web Credentials, Workspace themes, Export Application Component, Application Express Views and Manage Backups.

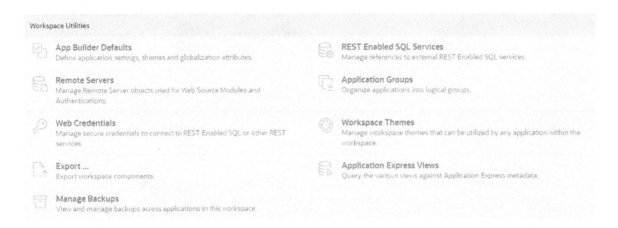

4.2 SQL WORKSHOP

SQL workshop provides us with a GUI (Graphical User Interface) for Viewing and managing database objects. It is further classified as with following features:

- Object Browser
- SQL Commands
- SQL Scripts
- Utilities
- RESTful Services

4.2.1 Object Browser

Drives to the page that has two panes, one is selection pane and the other one is the detail pane. The Selection pane enables the developer to browse through the database objects. The developer can use the search bar to narrow down the results and view the details of the purpose by using the tabs in the details pane for the selected object.

4.2.2 SQL Command

SQL Commandis a workplace where the developer can execute the SQL scripts/queries. The results of the query can be viewed in the result tab. It is also possible to get the explain plan of the query for tuning the performance. Besides, SQL Command workplace featured to save the SQL query for the future reference and uses. In case, if you forget to preserve the query, the history tab will help you to find the series of the executed query.

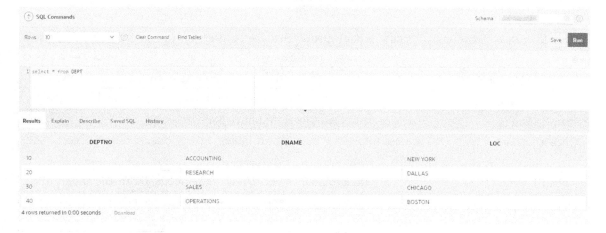

4.2.3 SQL Scripts

SQL Scripts is a workplace where we can create, edit, view, run and delete SQL script files. It also provides an option like export and imports the files from the current Script Repository to a Script Repository in a different workspace, manage results task to view and delete scripts result.

4.2.4 Utilities

There are different utilities in SQL workshop for various purposes of developers. The utilities and its purpose has been briefed as below:

UTILITIES	PURPOSE
Data Workshop	Data Workshop
Query Builder	Build queries graphically by adding tables to the panel and selecting the columns to be returned
Quick SQL	Generate SQL using the shorthand syntax
Sample Datasets	Install, refresh or remove sample datasets
Generate DDL	Generate scripts for all or selected database objects within a schema
User Interface Defaults	Specify layout properties to consistently generate items/columns across pages and applications
Schema Comparison	Show differences between database objects in two different schemas
Methods on Tables	Generate API scripts for DML operations on specified tables
Recycle Bin	Restore database objects that have been dropped
Object Reports	Access numerous reports on tables, exceptions, security, objects and PL/SQL code
About Database	Review database details. For this schema needs, DBA role is required
Database Monitor	Run database activity reports. For this schema needs, DBA role is required

The appearance of these utilities in the application shown below for the immediate reference:

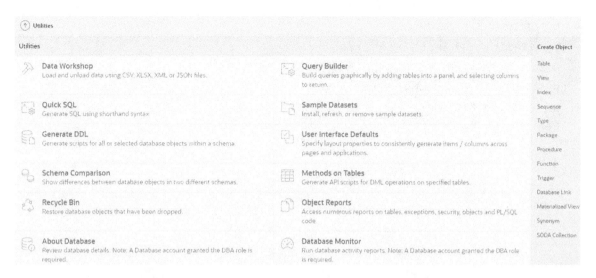

4.2.5 ORDS RESTful Services

ORDS is "Oracle RESTful Data Service" is a web service for electronic data transfer from one database to another; we can enable ORDS for the database using ORDS API. The ORDS can be enabled for the entire schema or for a specific table based on the requirement and this enhances the security of the database.

```
BEGIN
ORDS.enable_schema(
p_enabled            => TRUE,
p_schema             => 'TESTUSER1',
p_url_mapping_type   => 'BASE_PATH',
p_url_mapping_pattern => 'testuser1',
p_auto_rest_auth     => FALSE
  );
END;
```

We have different API's for services creations and methods like GET, PUT and DELETE for the data manipulation and review.

```
BEGIN
ORDS.define_service(
p_module_name   => 'testmodule1',
p_base_path     => 'testmodule1/',
```

```
p_pattern      => 'emp/',
p_method       => 'GET',
p_source_type  =>ORDS.source_type_collection_feed,
p_source       => 'SELECT * FROM emp',
p_items_per_page => 0);
END;
```

4.3 TEAM DEVELOPMENT

The Team Development home page is for managing and tracking the development activities of the application; we can split the application into different modules and add to the milestone and to-do list. The feedback is the place where the end user's feedback will be displayed to the developers.

The following large icons displayed on the Team Development home page:

- **Milestones:**Track events related to the development process and link milestones to features, bugs and to-dos.
- **Features**: Track features from the initial concept to implementation. You can organize features with releases, assignees, tags or associated milestones.
- **To Dos**: Manage actions that can be assigned, prioritized, taggedand tracked. The parent tasks may also be related to to-dos. Dosing may or may not be associated with a feature or milestone.
- **Bugs**: Track software defects or bugs. Bugs can be assigned, linked to milestones and tracked by the due date, status and other attributes.

- **Feedback:** Getting feedback, enhancement requests and bugs from your users in real-time.

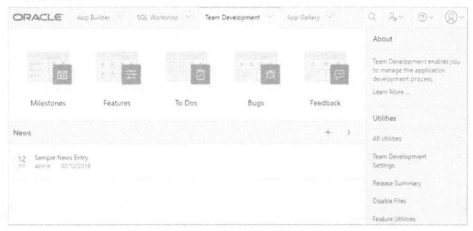

4.4 APP GALLERY

Oracle APEX provides a wide range of Productivity and Sample Applications (Packaged App). App Gallery drives the developers to view, install and run the packaged app to understand more about how to construct a distinct type of pages and applications.

There is a difference between the Sample application and Productivity application. The Sample applications are fully editable by default. On the other hand, you need to unlock productivity applications before you can edit them. Unlocking the productivity application makes it ineligible for future upgrades or support from Oracle Support.

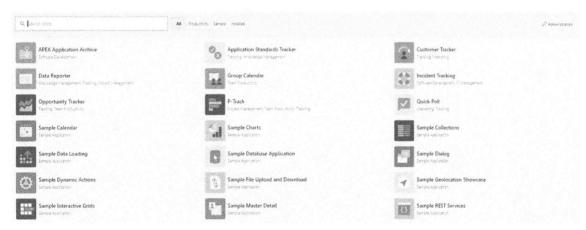

feedback or asking questions...

3.4 App Gallery

Oracle APEX provides a wide range of Productivity and Sample Applications (packaged Apps). App Gallery allows the developer to view, install and run the packaged app to understand more about how to construct a useful type of pages and applications.

There is a difference between Sample application and Productivity application. The sample applications are fully editable by default. On the other hand, you need to unlock productivity applications before customizing. Unlocking the productivity application enables multiple installation or support from Oracle support.

APEX PAGE COMPONENTS

A page is the basic building block of an application. When you build an application in App Builder, you create pages that contain user interface elements, such as tabs, lists, buttons, items and regions. Developers add pages to an existing database application by running the Create Page Wizard

To Tailor fit the APEX applications as per business needs, Let's explore a few scenarios of tailor fitting page components in the upcoming chapters.

5.1 REGIONS

A region serves as a container for content in an APEX page. A page can have several regions. The region template controls the appearance of the region, the size, border or a background color and type of fonts display. A region template also determines the standard placement for any buttons placed in region positions.

Regions can be used to group page controls (such as items or buttons). Regions display in sequence in the page template body or can be placed explicitly into region positions.

5.1.1 Breadcrumb

Introduction to Breadcrumb

A Breadcrumb is a hierarchical list of links that indicates where the user is within the application from a hierarchical perspective. It is useful for providing navigational context to end-users and an easy way to navigate back to the home. The application breadcrumb has a special location for placement and should be used with the Title Bar region template in most cases.

Learning Objective

Breadcrumbs are the second level of navigation at the top of each page, complementing other user interface elements such as tabs and lists. Upon the default functionality of breadcrumb, we can also customize the value in breadcrumb region. Below is the use case for it.

Use case for Breadcrumb

5.1.1.1 Requirement:

Let us consider we have a requirement to hold the button position at a stable place. Whenever we scroll the regions, the button remains in the same place,but the Breadcrumb region title should be in Scrolling state.

Solution

Let us see the step by step process to create new breadcrumb, lists and include the newly created breadcrumb to the Source.

Step 1: Go to Shared Components and Click on Breadcrumbs Link.

Step 2: Click "Create Breadcrumb" and enter the breadcrumb name as "Breadcrumbdev".

Step 3: Click "Create Breadcrumb Entry" and enter the below details.

- **Page**: 1
- **Parent Entry**: None (If you want to set the hierarchy then select the parent list)
- **Short Name**: Home
- **TargetPage**: 1

Step 4: In the same manner, create breadcrumb Entries for Employee Creation and Employee Address Details.

- For "Employee Creation", set the Parent Entry as "Home".
- For "Employee Address Details", set the Parent Entry as "Employee Creation".

Step 5: Create a new region, assign the type as "Breadcrumb". Assign the Breadcrumb source as "Breadcrumbdev".

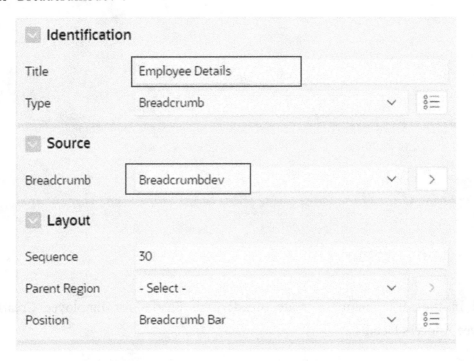

The layout position has been set as "Breadcrumb Bar".

Step 6: Create two new regions for Employee Form as a Static Content and Employee Details as an Interactive Report.

Step 7: Create a new item like Employee name, Emp no, Job and Department as a text field and assign to Employee Form Static Region.

Step 8: In Employee Details Interactive Report, place the below code in SQL Source.

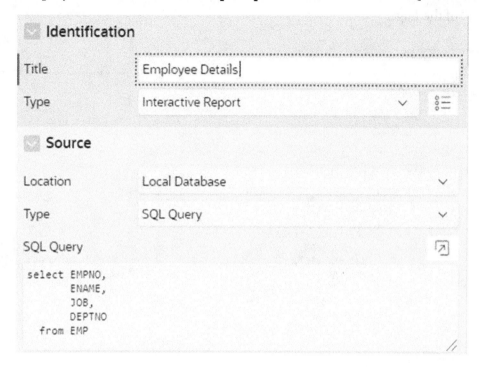

#Sample Code

select EMPNO, ENAME, JOB, DEPTNO from EMP;

Step 9: Create a submit Button and assign the breadcrumb region as "Employee Details".

Step 10: The below is the customize CSS code to scroll the breadcrumb title. Place the code in "Inline" of the Page.

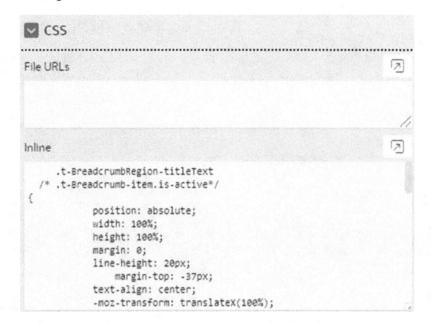

#Sample Code

```
.t-BreadcrumbRegion-titleText {
                position: absolute;
                width: 100%;
                height: 100%;
                margin: 0;
                line-height: 20px;
                margin-top: -37px;
                text-align: center;
                -moz-transform: translateX(100%);
                -webkit-transform: translateX(100%);
                transform: translateX(100%);
                -moz-animation: scroll-left 2s linear infinite;
                -webkit-animation: scroll-left 2s linear infinite;
                animation: scroll-left 20s linear infinite;
                color: red !important;
}
```

```
@-moz-keyframes scroll-left {
                0% {
                        -moz-transform: translateX(100%);
                }
                100% {
                        -moz-transform: translateX(-100%);
                }
}
@-webkit-keyframes scroll-left {
                0% {
                        -webkit-transform: translateX(100%);
                }
                100% {
                        -webkit-transform: translateX(-100%);
                }
}
@keyframes scroll-left {
                0% {
                        -moz-transform: translateX(100%);
                        -webkit-transform: translateX(100%);
                        transform: translateX(100%);
                }
                100% {
                        -moz-transform: translateX(-100%);
                        -webkit-transform: translateX(-100%);
                        transform: translateX(-100%);
                }
}
```

Output:

The below-highlighted portion is the list assigned to source as "Breadcrumbdev".

Here the Employee Details is the title for the Breadcrumb and it's in Scrolling State.

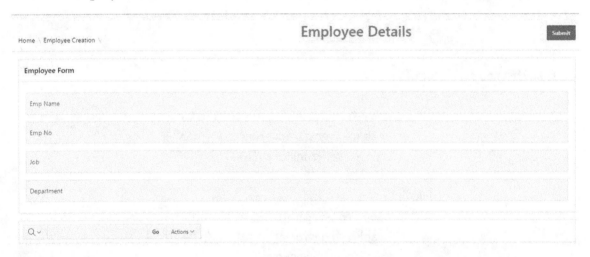

Here on scrolling to bottom of the Page, the button "Submit", is in Stable Position. It is not changed.

Employee Details   Submit

Empno	Ename	Job	Deptno
7839	KING	PRESIDENT	10
7698	BLAKE	MANAGER	30
7782	CLARK	MANAGER	10
7566	JONES	MANAGER	20
7788	SCOTT	ANALYST	20
7902	FORD	ANALYST	20
7369	SMITH	CLERK	20
7499	ALLEN	SALESMAN	30
7521	WARD	SALESMAN	30
7654	MARTIN	SALESMAN	30

5.1.2 Calendars

Introduction to Calendars

Calendar is a region component in Oracle APEX. This component helps to create events in 3 visual methods - like Weekly, Monthly, List. Oracle APEX supports 2 types of Calendars – Legacy Calendar and Calendar. As per 18.1 release statement from Oracle, legacy calendar is template based and may be deprecated in the future release. Calendar is based on Full Calendar jQuery library and can be customized using CSS.

Calendar component can be added to a region of a page using any of the following methods

- Create Page Wizard to create a new page with a calendar using a local database.
- Create Page Wizard to add a new page with a calendar that uses a remote database reference.
- Manually create a calendar in Page Designer by providing the SQL query.

Display of the created calendar component can also be altered by editing the two sets of editable attributes - region and calendar attributes.

Learning Objective

We can customize the calendar component using HTML and CSS. Below is a use case for Calendar:

The objective of this section is to explore and understand ways to effectively customize the calendar component using JavaScript, HTML and CSS.

Use case for Calendar:

For instance, let us consider the event of

- Changing background colors of display titles.
- Display the Table of Contents (instead of simple text content) during a mouse over event; Refer to samples.
- Navigate to specific date in calendar from a report or grid.

On mouse-over of the event/ display name, additional details will be displayed as shown below:

5.1.2.1 Requirement 1:

- Changing background colors of display titles.
- Display the Table of Contents (instead of simple text content) during a mouse over event; Refer to samples.

Solution:

We can achieve this using HTML and CSS in Calendar region. Let us see the step by step process to achieve this.

Step 1: Create a *Region* & select the *Type* as *Calendar* and *Source* type as "*SQL Query*".

#Sample Code

```
SELECT
sid,
student_name as display,
student_roll_number,
student_dob,
student_age,
schedule_date,
    CASE
        WHEN grade = 1   THEN 'apex-cal-green'
        WHEN grade = 2   THEN 'apex-cal-yellow'
        WHEN grade = 3   THEN 'apex-cal-red'
        WHEN grade = 4   THEN 'apex-cal-black'
    END CSS_CLASS
FROM   student_master;
```

In the SQL query, select any of the following default classes for the background color of the event/ display titles.

- *apex-cal-red*
- *apex-cal-cyan*
- *apex-cal-blue*
- *apex-cal-bluesky*
- *apex-cal-darkblue*
- *apex-cal-green*
- *apex-cal-yellow*
- *apex-cal-silver*
- *apex-cal-brown*
- *apex-cal-lime*
- *apex-cal-white*
- *apex-cal-gray*
- *apex-cal-black*
- *apex-cal-orange*

To style the event, add the CSS Class. Use the click paths as *Settings- >CSSClass* Section.

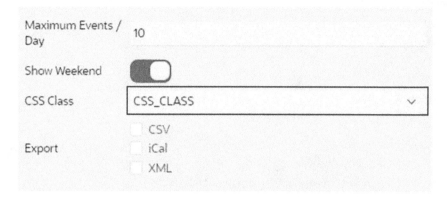

Step 2: Add the HTML script into the *Calendar -> Settings -> Supplemental Information* Section, to achieve the inline mouse over display.

```
<table width="50%" align="center" border="1">
        <div id="head_nav">
            <tr>
                <th>Time</th>
                <th>Monday</th>
                <th>Tuesday</th>
                <th>Wednesday</th>
                <th>Thrusday</th>
                <th>Friday</th>
                <th>Saturday</th>
            </tr>
            <tr>
                <th>10:00 - 11:00</th>
                <td>Applied Mathematics </td>
                <td>Computer Networks</td>
                <td>Information Theory and Coding</td>
                <td>Computer Organization and Architecture</td>
                <td>Automata Theory</td>
                <td>Web Programming</td>
            </tr>
```

#Sample Code

```
<table width="50%" align="center" border="1">
<div id="head_nav">
<tr>
<th>Time</th>
<th>Monday</th>
<th>Tuesday</th>
```

```
<th>Wednesday</th>
<th>Thrusday</th>
<th>Friday</th>
<th>Saturday</th>
</tr>
<tr>
<th>10:00 - 11:00</th>
<td>Applied Mathematics </td>
<td>Computer Networks</td>
<td>Information Theory and Coding</td>
<td>Computer Organization and Architecture</td>
<td>Automata Theory</td>
<td>Web Programming</td>
</tr>
<tr>
<th>11:00 - 12:00</th>
<td>Information Theory and Coding</td>
<td>Web Programming</td>
<td>Computer Networks</td>
<td>Computer Networks</td>
<td>Automata Theory</td>
<td>Applied Mathematics</td>
</tr>
</div>
</table>
```

To achieve the styles, include the below CSS in Page Inline Section.

```
table {font-family: arial, sans-serif;
border-collapse: collapse;
width: 100%;
}
td, th {
text-align: left;
padding: 2px;
font-size:11px;
}
tr:nth-child(even) {
background-color: #dddddd;
}
```

Output:

Now UI of the Calendar event with different color is as follows:

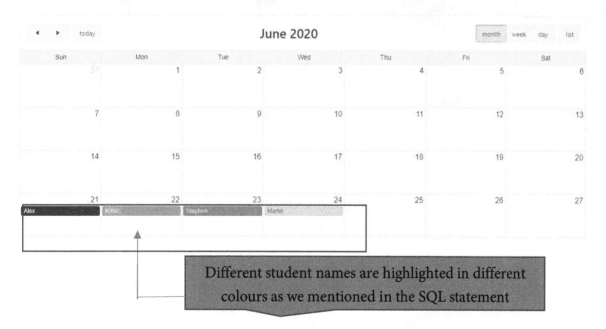

Different student names are highlighted in different colours as we mentioned in the SQL statement

On Mouse Over Dialog

On mouse over, the various schedules of Student "Stephen" has been displayed in tabular format

5.1.2.2   Requirement 2:

Navigate to specific date in calendar from a report or grid.

Solution:

This could be achieved using JavaScript. Let us see the step by step process for the same.

Step 1: Create Calendar page with the following query.

#Sample Code

```
SELECT *
  FROM STUDENT_MASTER
  WHERE SID = :P23_SID;
```

Step 2: Create a grid with link to the Calendar page and give static ID as **DOBCAL**, pass the date of birth date to page item **P23_date.**

Step 3: Place the JavaScript in the "Execute on page Load" calendar Page.

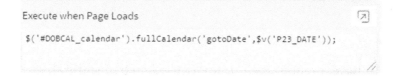

#Sample Code

$('#DOBCAL_calendar').fullCalendar('gotoDate',$v('P23_DATE'));

Output:

Now focus is shifted to the date passed:

5.1.3 Charts

Introduction to Charts

Charts allow to illustrate data graphically; they are often usedfor ease understanding of large quantities of data and explore/represent relationships between various data elements. Charts can usually be read more quickly than Textual data. Chart support in Oracle APEX is based on the Oracle JavaScript Extension Toolkit (Oracle JET) Data Visualizations.

Learning Objective

Oracle JET is a collection of open-source JavaScript libraries with a set of Oracle's contributed JavaScript libraries which helps to create Interactive charts easily. Since it's a graphical representation, we can also customize to call the charts dynamically. Below is the use case for charts.

Use case for Charts:

5.1.3.1 Requirement:

Let us consider we have a requirement to dynamically change the chart type for the same set of data. Refer to the below example:

In this table, we have Employee Jobs information and total employee count who has been assigned for this each job.

JOB	Count of Employees
Clerk	4
Manager	3
Salesman	3
Analyst	2
President	1

Using the above data, we can create a chart and see the steps to dynamically change the chart type.

Solution:

In Oracle JET there are many types of charts, now we are going to see the below chart types,

1. Pie Chart
2. Donut Chart
3. Funnel Chart
4. Pyramid Chart

First, Let's see the steps to create a simple Pie Chart and then see dynamically to change the chart type.

Step 1: Create static region and enter the region name as *Dynamic Chart I/P*.

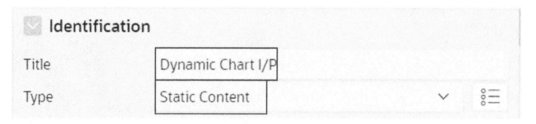

Step 2: Create a select list item in the name of **P18_CHART_TYPE** and choose list of value type as SQL query.

#Sample Code

```
SELECT  d, r
  FROM (SELECT 'Pie' d, 'pie' r, 1 seq
```

```
        FROM DUAL
    UNION
    SELECT 'Donut' d, 'donut' r, 2 seq
      FROM DUAL
    UNION
    SELECT 'Funnel' d, 'funnel' r, 3 seq
      FROM DUAL
    UNION
    SELECT 'Pyramid' d, 'pyramid' r, 4 seq
      FROM DUAL
    )
  ORDER BY seq
```

Step 3: Create a chart region and assign a Static ID as **DYN_CHRT** and Set Parent region as *Dynamic Chart I/P.*

Step 4:Click on Region attributes and Select the chart type as Pie and choose Value format as Decimal.

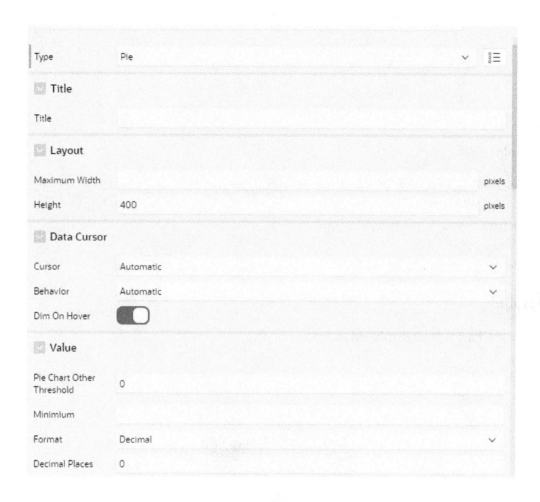

Step 5:Place the code given below in the query source and click Save.

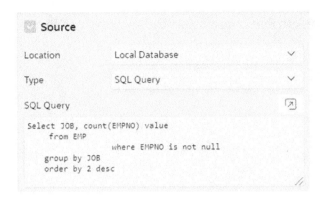

#*Sample Code*

```
Select JOB, count(EMPNO) value
 from EMP
where EMPNO is not null
group by JOB
order by 2 desc
```

Output:

Now the Chart will be displayed as below:

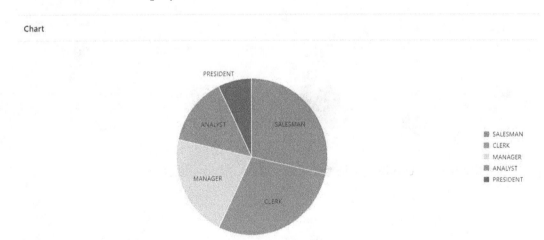

Now let's see how to add the JavaScript code for changing chart type dynamically.

Step 6: Create a dynamic action as follows,

Event: Change

SelectionType: Items(s)

Item(s): P18_CHART_TYPE

*Step 7:*Action: Execute JavaScript Code

Fire on Initialization: Yes

Click Save and Run the Page.

#Sample Code

```
var chrt = $('#P18_CHART_TYPE').val();
var chrt_typ2 = ["funnel", "pie", "pyramid", "donut"];
if (chrt_typ2.indexOf(chrt) >= 0) {
  apex.region('DYN_CHRT').widget().ojChart({
  styleDefaults: {
      'threeDEffect': 'on'
  }
```

```
});
if (chrt == "pie") {
apex.region('DYN_CHRT').widget().ojChart({
   type: chrt
});
apex.region("DYN_CHRT").widget().ojChart({
styleDefaults: {
pieInnerRadius: '0'
}
});
} else if (chrt == "donut") {
    apex.region('DYN_CHRT').widget().ojChart({
     type: "pie"
});
apex.region("DYN_CHRT").widget().ojChart({
styleDefaults: {
   pieInnerRadius: '0.5'
}
});
} else {
    apex.region('DYN_CHRT').widget().ojChart({
    type: chrt
   });
}}
```

Output:

1. *Chart Type: Donut*

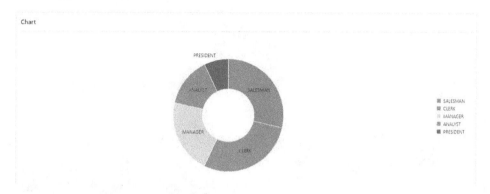

2. *Chart Type: Funnel*

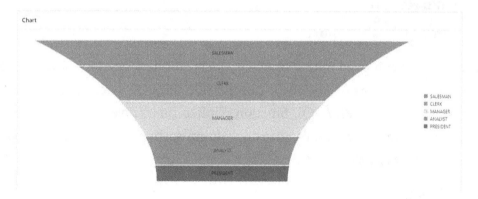

3. *Chart Type: Pie*

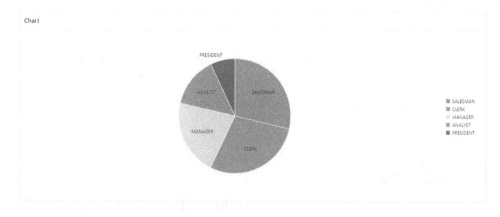

4. Chart Type: Pyramid

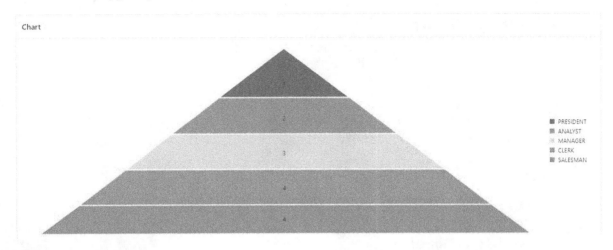

5.1.4 Classic Report

Introduction to Classic Report

A classic report is a compiled output of a SQL query. It offers developers to choose a table on which to build a report or provide a custom SQL SELECT statement or return a SQL SELECT statement with a PL / SQL function. Unlike Interactive Report, only developers have the control of report layout, pagination, column sorting, error messages, export links and column break of Classic reports.

Learning Objective

Generally, the Classic report in Oracle APEX is visualized as a typical tabular layout of data. But in reality,

Classic Report is a versatile component because it is a template-driven. Developers can design their own template to display the data in the UI. Let's see the use case of customizing the default template in the Classic Report.

Use case for Classic Report:

5.1.4.1 Requirement 1

Merge cells of multiple rows having the same value within a single column.

From the example given below, the column **Department** has value repeated in the table. We can merge values with "Accounting" as a merged cell and similarly for "Research".

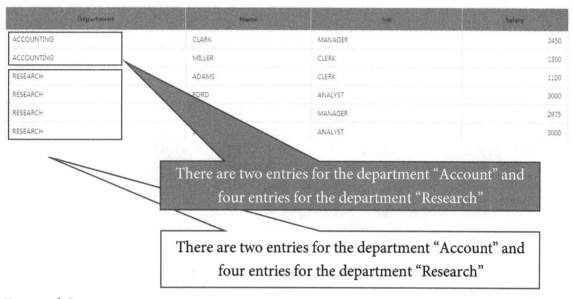

Expected Output:

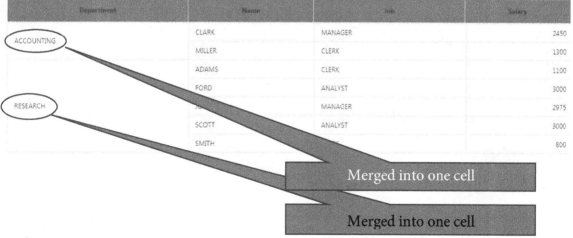

Solution:

You could achieve this by adding minimal JavaScript in Oracle APEX Dynamic Action. Let us see the step by step process to achieve this:

Step 1: Create a region in the name **Employee Report** and select region type as *Classic Report*.

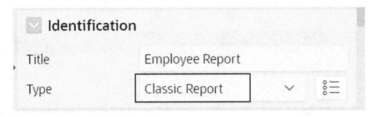

Step 2: Select source type as SQL Query and place your code:

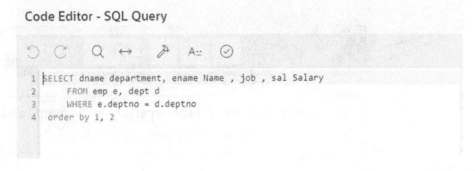

#Sample Code

```
SELECT dname department, enameName , job , sal Salary
FROM emp e, dept d
WHERE e.deptno = d.deptno
ORDER BY 1, 2
```

Step 3: Assign a static id as **EMP_RPT.**

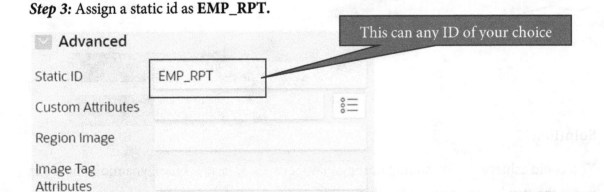

Step 4: Create a dynamic action using,

>Event :**After Refresh**

>Selection Type :**Region**

>Region :**Employee Report(report region)**

>Action :**Execute JavaScript Code**

>Fire on Initialization :**Yes**

#Sample Code

```
$("#report_EMP_RPT").each(function() {
   var $int_td, cur_val = "",
int_val = "",
hdr_cnt = "";
   $(this).find("td[headers='DEPARTMENT']").each(function() {
cur_val = $(this).text();
      if (int_val == "") {
int_val = cur_val;
        $int_td = $(this);
hdr_cnt = 1;
     } else if (int_val != cur_val) {
int_val = cur_val;
        $int_td.attr("rowspan", hdr_cnt);
        $int_td = $(this);
hdr_cnt = 1;
     } else if (int_val == cur_val) {
hdr_cnt++;
        $(this).remove();
     }
  });
  if (hdr_cnt != "") {
     $int_td.attr("rowspan", hdr_cnt);
  }
});
```

Step 5: Save and Run the page.

Output:

Now UI of the merged row is as follows:

Department	Name	Job	Salary
ACCOUNTING	CLARK	MANAGER	2450
	MILLER	CLERK	1300
	ADAMS	CLERK	1100
	FORD	ANALYST	3000
RESEARCH	JONES	MANAGER	2975
	SCOTT	ANALYST	3000
	SMITH	CLERK	800

5.1.4.2   Requirement 2:

Usually, when scrolling to the end of a classic report, the column headings would scroll up and hence the heading is not visible.

Solution:

We can implement a **Sticky Column header** to freeze or fix the column heading so that it is visible when scrolling the classic report. To accomplish this functionality, we can include JavaScript in Oracle APEX Dynamic Action. Let us see the step by step process to achieve this:

Step 1: Create a simple classic report.

Step 2: Place code given below in the JavaScript File URLs. (***This step is not required if APEX version is APEX 5.1.1.00.08***).
#Sample Code

```
#IMAGE_PREFIX#libraries/apex/#MIN_DIRECTORY#widget.stickyTableHeader#MIN#.js?v=#APEX_VERSION#
```

Step 3: Then Create dynamic action as follows:

Event: After Refresh

48

SelectionType: Region

Region: {select your classic report region}

Action: Execute JavaScript code

Fire on Initialization: Yes

#Sample Code

```
var vRegion$ = $(this.triggeringElement);
vRegion$.setTableHeadersAsFixed();
vRegion$.find('.js-stickyTableHeader').stickyWidget();
```

Step 4: Save and Run the page.

Note:Tested on APEX 5.1.1.00.08 and 18.*

Source for Requirement 2: http://apexbyg.blogspot.com/2017/04/how-to-make-any-table-header-sticky.html

5.1.5 Form

Introduction to Form

Form Regions enable user to load and submit the data that are linked to the table columns from a single table. The forms are created by two different methods either we can create manually or we can create at the time of Page Creation.

Learning Objective

The Form renders the source table that are defined in three different methods like Local Database, Rest Enabled SQL Service. However, the most used method is using the Local Database in our business applications. Since the forms are automatically created when we set the source table name, we can also customize the Form display mode. Below is the use case for it.

Use case for Form:

5.1.5.1 *Requirement:*

Let us consider a requirement, we have an employee form, that form style need to be customized with Border details. Below are the steps to create a simple form in two different methods and add the customization for the manually created form.

Solution:

5.1.5.1.1 Form Created at the time of Page Creation (Method 1):

Step 1:Select Form on Create a new Page.

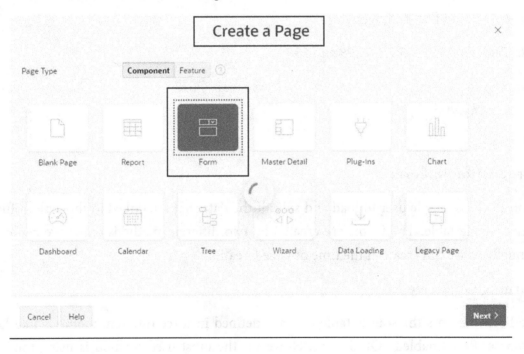

Step 2: Select Report with Form option.

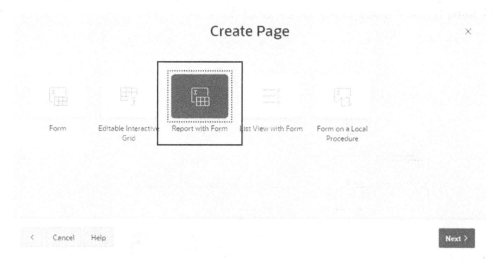

Step 3: Provide the mandatory information's required to create a form and in the below wizard.

Step 4: Provide the "Data Source" parameter's, such as "Source Type", "Table / View Owner" name (schema name) and the name of the table or view.

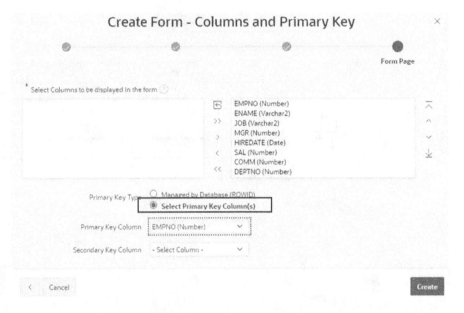

Step 5: Set the Primary Key of the table.

Step 6:Click and Run the Page. The Automatic Row Processing will be created automatically. Now the user can create and edit the employee details directly. Below is the interactive report that is created and click the link to redirect to "Edit" form.

	Empno	Ename	Job	Mgr	Hiredate	Sal	Comm	Deptno
	7839	KING	PRESIDENT		11/17/1981	5000		10
	7698	BLAKE	MANAGER	7839	5/1/1981	2850		30
	7782	CLARK	MANAGER	7839	6/9/1981	2450		10
	7566	JONES	MANAGER	7839	4/2/1981	2975		20
	7788	SCOTT	ANALYST	7566	12/9/1982	3000		20
	7902	FORD	ANALYST	7566	12/3/1981	3000		20
	7369	SMITH	CLERK	7902	12/17/1980	800		20
	7499	ALLEN	SALESMAN	7698	2/20/1981	1600	300	30
	7521	WARD	SALESMAN	7698	2/22/1981	1250	500	30
	7654	MARTIN	SALESMAN	7698	9/28/1981	1250	1400	30
	7844	TURNER	SALESMAN	7698	9/8/1981	1500	0	30
	7876	ADAMS	CLERK	7788	1/12/1983	1100		20

	Empno	Ename	Job
	7839	KING	PRESIDENT
	7698	BLAKE	MANAGER
	7782	CLARK	MANAGER
	7566	JONES	MANAGER
	7788	SCOTT	ANALYST
	7902	FORD	ANALYST

Link to go to "Edit" form

Step 7:In the Form edit region, we can edit the employee details and save it.

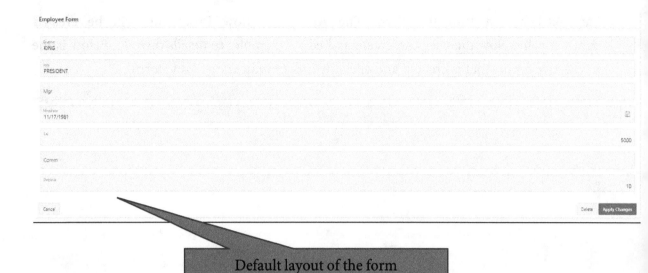

Default layout of the form

5.1.5.1.2 Form Created Manually (Method 2):

Step 1: Create a new region and set the type as "Form".

Step 2: Set the Source type as below.

Location: Local Database

Type: Table/View

Table Owner: Parsing Schema

Table Name: EMP

Include Row ID: Yes

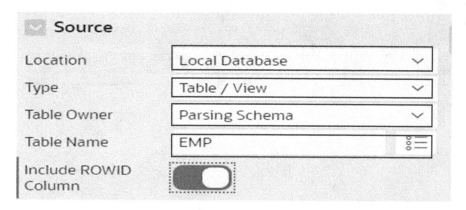

The Corresponding Emp table fields will be created automatically under the Form Region. We need to create the PL/SQL Process manually to update the Employee Details.

Step 3: Create the Customization for adding the Border Details for the Employee. Place the below code in the "*Inline*" of the Page.

#Sample Code

```
.container{
   border: 21px solid transparent;
   -webkit-border-image: url(#APP_IMAGES#Goldenborder.png) 30 round; /* Safari 3.1-
5 */
   -o-border-image: url(#APP_IMAGES#Goldenborder.png   ) 30 round; /* Opera 11-12.1
*/
   border-image: url(#APP_IMAGES#Form-border.jpg   ) 30 round;
}
```

//The below CSS is used to align the Form title in the Center and increase the font size.

```
.t-Region-title{
   margin-left: 45%;
   font-size: 140%;
}
```

The images are uploaded in the *Shared Components -> Static Application Files.*

Output:

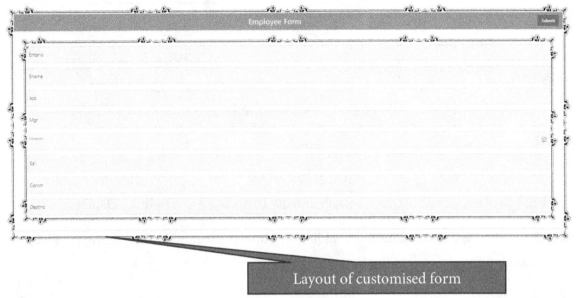

Layout of customised form

5.1.6 Interactive Grid

Introduction to Interactive grid

Interactive grid is a combination of forms and interactive report. Interactive grid includes most of the functionality of Interactive Report along with additional features, thereby presents users a set of data ina searchable, customizable report. Refer below image:

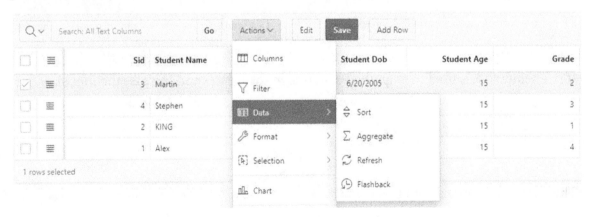

An editable interactive grid allows users to add, modify and refresh the data set directly on the page. Editable interactive grids also include additional controls. A Row Actions menu displays at the start of each row and enables users to add, edit and refresh rows. To the right of the Actions menu, additional buttons Edit, Save and Add Row is also provided. Refer below image:

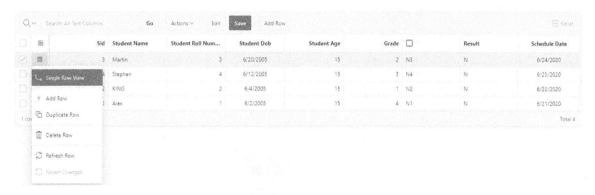

Learning Objective

The interactive grid displays the table data in the excel format and it also enables the user to edit and save the displayed data which provide a more robust toolset for directly editing data, as it can be modified and saved. There are also options like copying existing row data to a new row, delete a row and refresh row. Refresh row plays an important role, this enables the user to update the latest values from the table. As we know if a user is editing a row in Oracle, it locks the particular row for and releases the lock once commit for the change is done.

Use Case for Interactive Grid

5.1.6.1 Requirement:

Let's get the value from the grid column of the selected rows and assign the same to a page item. This could be achieved using JavaScript. Below is the approach:

Solution:

Step1: Create the Interactive grid based on the following query in the "*Source*".

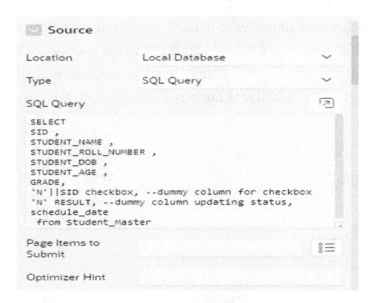

#Sample Code

```
SELECT SID,STUDENT_NAME,STUDENT_ROLL_NUMBER,STUDENT_DOB
,STUDENT_AGE,GRADE,RESULT,SCHEDULE_DATE
  FROM STUDENT_MASTER
```

Step 2: Create Dynamic action on the *Selection Change* event and type as region and select the Interactive grid region.

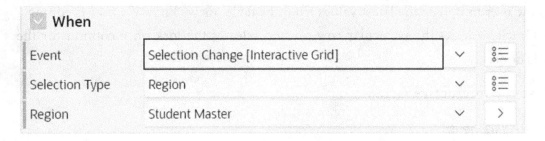

Step 3: Create True action to execute the JavaScript code given below.

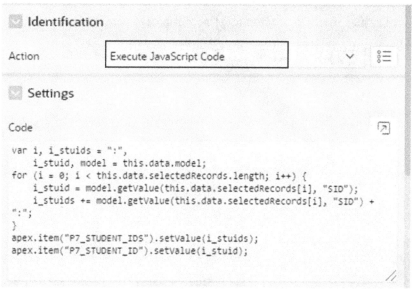

#*Sample Code*

```
var i, i_stuids = ":",
i_stuid, model = this.data.model;
for (i = 0; i<this.data.selectedRecords.length; i++) {
i_stuid = model.getValue(this.data.selectedRecords[i], "SID");
i_stuids += model.getValue(this.data.selectedRecords[i], "SID") + ":";
}
apex.item("P7_STUDENT_IDS").setValue(i_stuids);
apex.item("P7_STUDENT_ID").setValue(i_stuid);
```

Output:

Based on the selection of the row selector the selected records will be assigned to the corresponding items.

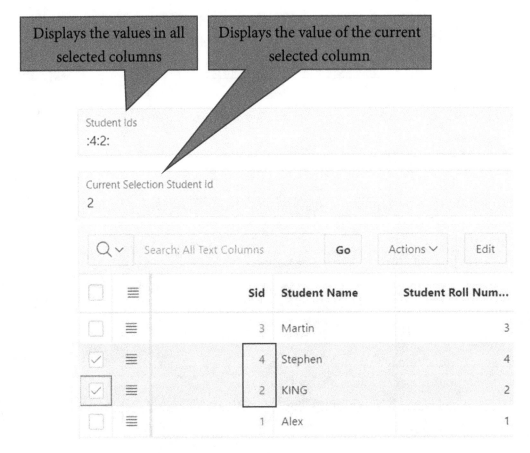

5.1.7 Interactive Report

Introduction to Interactive Report

An Interactive report is a structured output of a SQL query. The Create Application Wizard and Create Page Wizard supports the creation of Interactive report. An Interactive report offers developers to choose a table on which to build a report or provide a custom SQL SELECT statement. End-users can modify the style of the report and the data shown by using various options from the Action menu.

The interactive reporting region allows users to customize the data layout by selecting the columns they're interested in, applying filters, highlighting and sorting. They can also define breaks, aggregations, different charts and their own calculations.

Learning Objective

Above the default functionality, the APEX developer can also customize the Interactive Report. Let's see two different use cases given below:

Use case for Interactive Report:

5.1.7.1 Requirement 1:

When there is a requirement to change the department of an employee and store the changes in the database from IR report layout. In addition to that, include cascading select list option in the IR report layout to list the employee belonging to the selected department. Let's see how we can do this.

(Note: Making Interactive Report editable enables the Users to use all the functionality available in it as well as allowing them to do the modification in the existing dataset and store it in the database. This will be useful in the older version where tabular form presents. Customizing Interactive Report to make editable might not be required in the APEX versions that have an Interactive Grid.)

Solution:

We can achieve this by adding minimal JavaScript/PLSQL code in Oracle APEX Dynamic Action. Let us see the step by step process to achieve this:

Step 1: Create a region in the name **Employee IR Report** and select region *type* as *InteractiveReport*.

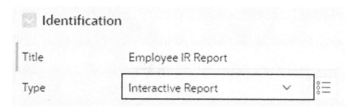

Step 2: Select *source* type as SQL Query and place the code.

```
Code Editor - SQL Query
↺  ↻  Q  ↔  ↗  A≡  ⊘

1  SELECT apex_item.checkbox (1,empno,NULL,NULL,NULL,'f01_' || ROWNUM) || apex_item.hidden (2, 'N', p_item_id => 'f02_' || ROWNUM) chkbx,
2  empno, apex_item.select_list_from_query (10,p.deptno,'select DNAME   , DEPTNO from DEPT','onchange="f_set_casc_sel_list_item(this,''f11_'|| LPAD (ROWNUM, 4, '0')|| ''')"'
3             'YES', '', '- Select DNAME -', 'f10_' || LPAD (ROWNUM, 4, '0'), NULL,'NO') dname,
4      apex_item.select_list_from_query (11, a.ENAME,'SELECT DISTINCT ENAME d,'|| 'ENAME r FROM EMP where DEPTNO = '|| a.deptno,'','YES','','- Select User -',
5             'f11_' || LPAD (ROWNUM, 4, '0'),NULL,'NO') ename,
6      apex_item.text (12, a.sal, p_item_id => 'f12_' || ROWNUM) sal
7  FROM emp a, dept b
8  WHERE a.deptno = b.deptno
```

#Sample Code

```
SELECT   apex_item.checkbox (1, empno, NULL, NULL, NULL, 'f01_' || ROWNUM)
      || apex_item.hidden (2, 'N', p_item_id => 'f02_' || ROWNUM) chkbx,
empno,
apex_item.select_list_from_query
          (10,
b.deptno,
          'select DNAME , DEPTNO from DEPT',
            'onchange="f_set_casc_sel_list_item(this,''f11_'
          || LPAD (ROWNUM, 4, '0')
          || ''')"',
          'YES',
          '',
          '- Select DNAME -',
          'f10_' || LPAD (ROWNUM, 4, '0'),
          NULL,
          'NO'
          ) dname,
apex_item.select_list_from_query
              (11,
a.ENAME,
              'SELECT DISTINCT ENAME d, '
              || 'ENAME r FROM EMP where DEPTNO = '
              || a.deptno,
              '',
              'YES',
              '',
```

```
                    '- Select User -',
                    'f11_' || LPAD (ROWNUM, 4, '0'),
                    NULL,
                    'NO'
                    ) ename,
    apex_item.text (12, a.sal, p_item_id => 'f12_' || ROWNUM) sal
       FROM emp a, dept b
     WHERE a.deptno = b.deptno
```

Step 3: Set **Escape special characters** as **"No"** for the following Columns **CHKBX, DNAME, ENAME, SAL.**

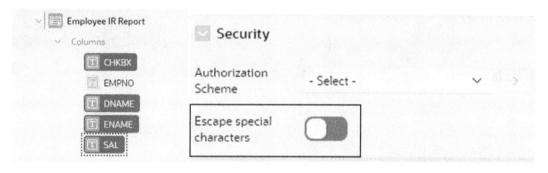

Step 4: Create a button named as SAVE.

Step 5: In the Page header ->*Function and Global Variable Declaration*, type in the below code as displayed in the screen shot:

Code Editor - Function and Global Variable Declaration

```
1  function f_set_casc_sel_list_item(a, b) {
2      var p_deptno = $(a).val();
3      apex.server.process('GET_EMP_FR_DEPT', {
4          x01: p_deptno
5      }, {
6          success: function(pData) {
7              var ret = pData;
8              $('#' + b).children('option:not(:first)').remove();
9              if (ret) {
10                 $("#" + b).append(ret);
11             }
12         },
13         dataType: "text"
14     });
15 }
```

#Sample Code

```
function f_set_casc_sel_list_item(a, b) {
   var p_deptno = $(a).val();
apex.server.process('GET_EMP_FR_DEPT', {
    x01: p_deptno
  }, {
    success: function(pData) {
       var ret = pData;
       $('#' + b).children('option:not(:first)').remove();
       if (ret) {
          $("#" + b).append(ret);
       }
    },
dataType: "text"
   });
}
```

Step 6: Create a *Dynamic action* on the page.

Event: Change

SelectionType: jQuery Selector

jQuerySelector: [name=f01]

Action: Execute JavaScript Code

Fireon Initialization: Yes

#Sample Code

```
var column_id = this.triggeringElement.id;
var rw_id = column_id.substr(4);
if ($("#"+column_id).is(":checked")) {
    $('#f02_'+rw_id).val('Y');
} else {
    $('#f02_'+rw_id).val('N');
}
```

Step 7: Create a *page process* on the page to store the changes in the database.

Code Editor - PL/SQL Code

```
 1  DECLARE
 2      lv_seq_id    VARCHAR2 (4000);
 3      cnt          NUMBER            := 0;
 4      lv_query     VARCHAR2 (32000);
 5  BEGIN
 6      FOR i IN 1 .. apex_application.g_f02.COUNT
 7      LOOP
 8          IF (apex_application.g_f02 (i) = 'Y')
 9          THEN
10              BEGIN
11                  UPDATE emp
12                      SET ename = apex_application.g_f11 (i),
13                          deptno = apex_application.g_f10 (i),
14                          sal = apex_application.g_f12 (i)
15                      WHERE empno = apex_application.g_f01 (i);
16              END;
17          END IF;
18      END LOOP;
19  END;
```

#*Sample Code*

```
DECLARE
lv_seq_id  VARCHAR2 (4000);
cnt        NUMBER       := 0;
lv_query   VARCHAR2 (32000);
BEGIN
  FOR i IN 1 .. apex_application.g_f02.COUNTLOOP
    IF (apex_application.g_f02 (i) = 'Y') THEN
      BEGIN
        UPDATE emp
          SET ename = apex_application.g_f11 (i),
deptno = apex_application.g_f10 (i),
sal = apex_application.g_f12 (i)
          WHERE empno = apex_application.g_f01 (i);
END;
    END IF;
  END LOOP;
END;
```

Step 8: Save the changes done in the page designer.

Step 9: Navigate to the *Shared Components* and click *Application process* to create a *Ajax call back* process and enter the process name as *GET_EMP_FR_DEPT* and place the code given below:

Shared Components ==> Application Process

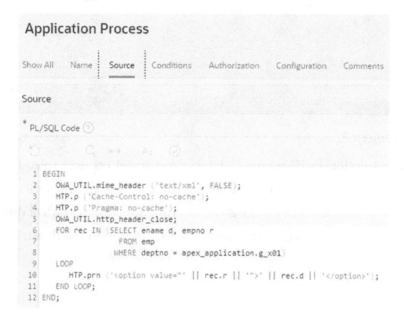

#*Sample Code*

```
BEGIN
OWA_UTIL.mime_header ('text/xml', FALSE);
HTP.p ('Cache-Control: no-cache');
HTP.p ('Pragma: no-cache');
OWA_UTIL.http_header_close;
  FOR rec IN (SELECT ename d, empno r
        FROM emp
        WHERE deptno = apex_application.g_x01)
  LOOP
HTP.prn ('<option value="' || rec.r || '">' || rec.d || '</option>');
  END LOOP;
END;
```

Step 10: Save and Run the page.

Output:

Empno	Department		Ename		Salary	Chkbx
7839	SALES	∨	King	∨	5000	☐
7698	SALES	∨	BLAKE	∨	2850	☐
7782	ACCOUNTING	∨	CLARK	∨	2450	☐
7566	RESEARCH	∨	JONES	∨	2975	☐
7788	RESEARCH	∨	SCOTT	∨	3000	☐

5.1.7.2 Requirement 2:

Default download option in IR report to be enabled based on user role. That is to enable download option in the IR report if the user has Admin Role and for others, the download option should be disabled. From APEX 20.0, this functionality to control download option to enable/disable, can be achieved by adding an authorization to the IR attribute.

Refer below screenshot for APEX 20.0

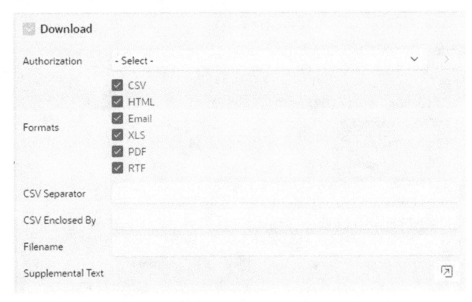

Let's see how to achieve this in the earlier versions.

Step 1: Click **Shared Components** and navigate to **Authorization Schemes.** Then, Create an *Authorization scheme* to validate the user role returning Boolean type.

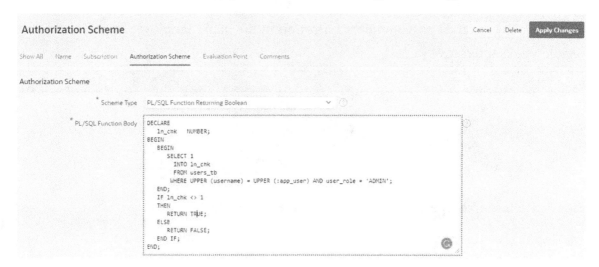

Name: Administration Rights

Type: PL/SQL Function Returning Boolean.

Code:

#Sample Code

```
DECLARE
ln_chkNUMBER;
BEGIN
  BEGIN
    SELECT 1
     INTO ln_chk
     FROM users_tb   --(replace with your table)
     WHERE UPPER (username) = UPPER (:app_user) AND user_role = 'ADMIN';
END;
  IF ln_chk<> 1
  THEN
    RETURN FALSE;
```

```
  ELSE
    RETURN TRUE;
  END IF;
END;
```

Step 2: Go to the target page and create a region in the name Employee Report and select region type as Interactive Report.

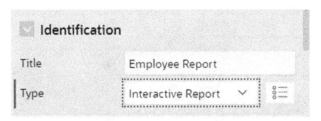

Step 3: Select source type as SQL Query and place your code.

#Sample Code

```
SELECT dname department, enameName , job , sal Salary
 FROM emp e, dept d
 WHERE e.deptno = d.deptno
 order by 1, 2
```

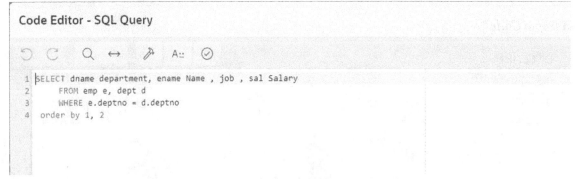

Step 4: Assign a static id as **EMP_RPT.**

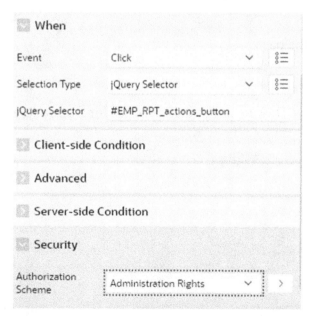

Step 5: Create a dynamic action using:

Event: Click

Selection Type: jQuery Selector

jQuery Selector: #EMP_RPT_actions_button

Region: Employee Report(report region)

Authorization Scheme: Administration Rights(refer step 1)

Action: Execute JavaScript Code

Fire on Initialization: No

#Sample Code

```
setTimeout(function(){
$( ".icon-irr-download" ).parent().parent().parent().parent().prev().remove();
$( ".icon-irr-download" ).parent().parent().parent().parent().remove();
}, 100);
```

Step 6: Save and Run the page.

Output:

In the below screen shot Download option is enabled for Admin Role.

In the below screen shot Download option is disabled for roles other than Admin role.

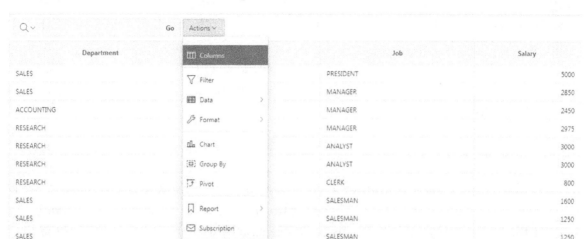

5.1.8 List

Introduction to List

The List component is a collection of links which can be used for navigation and other action-oriented tasks. A list will be available under Navigation region on the Shared Components and it can be created globally and associate any of the pages within the application. Appearance of the List is controlled through List templates. Each list can be controlled by adding a display condition to it. List can optionally show badges, icons, sub-list items and more.

Two types of lists can be created in Oracle APEX,

- Static Lists
- Dynamic Lists

Static List

The Static List is based on the predefined values for display and return. When creating a static list, you define a list entry label and a target (either a page or a URL). When you create a list, you can add list entries (building from scratch), copy existing entries or add list entries. You can control the display of list entries by defining the display conditions.

Dynamic List

The Dynamic List is based on a SQL query or a PL/SQL function that is executed at runtime. A dynamic list allows you to create stylized list items that support mobile frameworks dynamically. The list definition shows a specific type of page items, such as progress bars, sidebars, navigation bars or navigation menus. You can use templates to control how a list display.

Learning Objective

Oracle APEX provides a standard set of templates like Badge list, Cards, Links List, Media List, Menu Bar and more to the list. However, the developers can also change the Look and Feel of the list by applying CSS. Let us see a use case by applying CSS to change the look and feel of the list.

Use case for Static List:

5.1.8.1 Requirement 1:

To change the look and feel of the list from the standard template.

Solution:

You could achieve this by adding CSS in Oracle APEX. Let us see the step by step process to achieve this.

Step 1: Go to the application *Shared components* and navigate to Navigation section and select the item list and click create button to create the List.

Step 2: Mention whether to create the list *'Fromscratch'* or *'As a Copy of an existing list'*. (For an example, here we choose an option from scratch and click next)

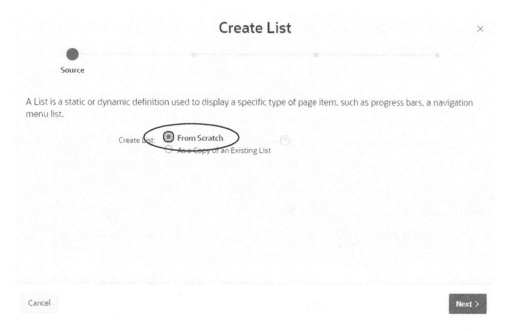

Step 3: Enter the name of the list and for an example, here we choose *Static* option among the Static/ Dynamic options and click next.

Step 4: Define a list entry and click next.

Step 5: Choose '*Create list region for each target page*' and click '*Create*'. Now the list will be created on each target page by default.

Step 6: Navigate to the target page and Run the page. Below screen shot is an example how the list looks like when we choose the standard template as **Tabs**.

Ename	Dname	Job	Empno	Hiredate	Loc
JONES	RESEARCH	MANAGER	7566	4/2/1981	DALLAS
KING	ACCOUNTING	PRESIDENT	7839	11/17/1981	NEW YORK
MARTIN	SALES	SALESMAN	7654	9/28/1981	CHICAGO
MILLER	ACCOUNTING	CLERK	7934	1/23/1982	NEW YORK
SCOTT	RESEARCH	ANALYST	7788	12/9/1982	DALLAS
SMITH	RESEARCH	CLERK	7369	12/17/1980	DALLAS
TURNER	SALES	SALESMAN	7844	9/8/1981	CHICAGO
WARD	SALES	SALESMAN	7521	2/22/1981	CHICAGO

1 - 14

Employee Detail   Department Detail

Step 7: Now let us see how to change the standard look and feel by applying CSS code. Go back to the *pagedesigner* and click on the list and navigate to *Advanced* section in the property of the list region and assign a static id as **EMP_LIST**.

Advanced

Static ID   EMP_LIST

Custom Attributes

Region Image

Image Tag
Attributes

Step 8: Click page title and navigate to CSS section and type in the below given code in the *Inline*.

```
   CSS

File URLs                                    ↗



Inline                                       ↗
    color: white;
    text-align: center;
    padding: 14px 16px;
    text-decoration: none;
}

#EMP_LIST li a:hover {
    background-color: #111;
}
#EMP_LIST .t-Tabs-label {
    color:white;
}
```

#Sample Code

```css
#EMP_LIST ul {
   list-style-type: none;
   margin: 0;
   padding: 0;
   overflow: hidden;
   background-color: #333;
}
#EMP_LIST li {
   float: left;
}
#EMP_LIST li a {
   display: block;
   color: white;
   text-align: center;
   padding: 14px 16px;
   text-decoration: none;
}
#EMP_LIST li a:hover {
   background-color: #111;
```

```
}
#EMP_LIST .t-Tabs-label {
color:white;
}
```

Step 9: Save and Run the Page.

Output:

Employee Detail	Department Detail					
Q∨		Go	Actions ∨			>
Ename	**Dname**	**Job**	**Empno**	**Hiredate**	**Loc**	
ADAMS	RESEARCH	CLERK	7876	1/12/1983	DALLAS	
ADAMS	RESEARCH	CLERK	7876	1/12/1983	DALLAS	
ADAMS	RESEARCH	CLERK	7876	1/12/1983	DALLAS	
ADAMS	RESEARCH	CLERK	7876	1/12/1983	DALLAS	
ADAMS	RESEARCH	CLERK	7876	1/12/1983	DALLAS	
ADAMS	RESEARCH	CLERK	7876	1/12/1983	DALLAS	
ADAMS	RESEARCH	CLERK	7876	1/12/1983	DALLAS	
ADAMS	RESEARCH	CLERK	7876	1/12/1983	DALLAS	

5.1.9 List View

Introduction to List View

List view is optimized for data display and smart phone navigation. List view on a page contains the formatted result of a SQL query. Developers could provide a custom SQL SELECT statement or a return SQL Query PL/SQL function.

Learning Objective

Reporting is a common way of displaying information on the Oracle APEX page. Report will generally display as a table that consists of rows and columns. There is limited room for displaying tabular information on the smart phone screen. A list view is ideal for this purpose.

Use case for List View:

5.1.9.1 Requirement:

Let's look at the example of creating a more informative list view by displaying Classic/IR report based on the value chosen in the list view.

Solution:

You could achieve this by adding simple HTML code in the target page of the Oracle APEX. Let us see the step by step process to achieve this.

Step 1: Create a region in the name **Department** and select region type as **List View**.

Step 2: Select the source type as Table/View and choose DEPT table.

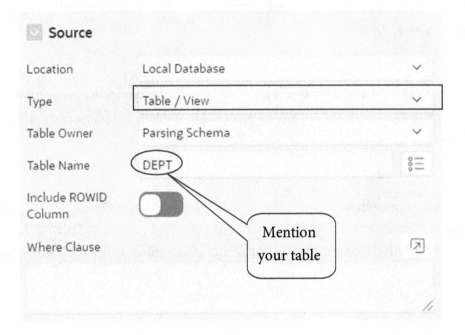

Step 3: Go to List view attribute.

Step 4: Now choose "*Advanced Formatting*" available in the Setting section.

Step 5: Text Formatting column will be enabled, then type in the below given code.

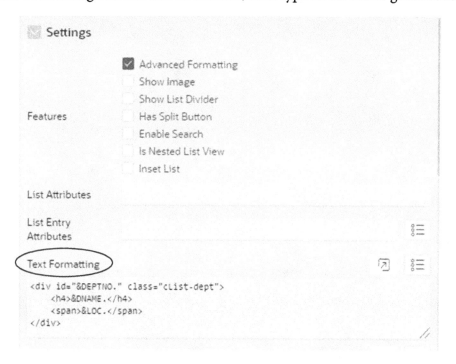

#Sample Code

```
<div id="&DEPTNO." class="cList-dept">
<h4>&DNAME.</h4>
<span>&LOC.</span>
</div>
```

Step 6: Click on page title and navigate to the CSS section and type in the below code in the *Inline.*

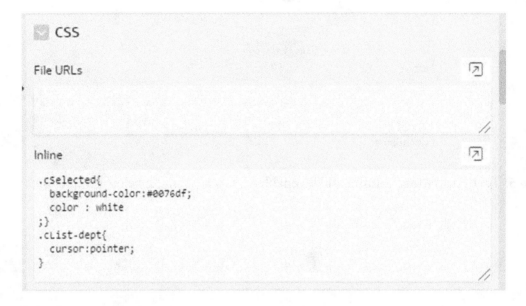

#Sample Code

```
.cSelected{
  background-color:#0076df;
color : white;
}
.cList-dept{
cursor:pointer;
}
```

Step 7: Create the **hidden item** in the name of PX_DEPT.

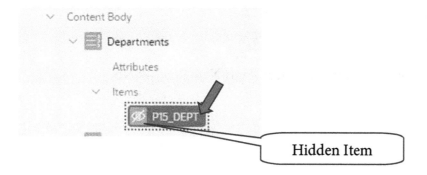

Hidden Item

Step 8: Create a region in the name **Employee Report** and select region type as Classic Report.

Step 9: Select source type as SQL Query and place your code.

```
SELECT
e.empno,e.ename,e.job,e.sal,e.mgr,e.hiredate,d.dname
FROM emp e, dept d
where e.deptno= d.deptno
and d.deptno = :P15_DEPT
ORDER by ename
```

#Sample Code

```
SELECT e.empno,e.ename,e.job,e.sal,e.mgr,e.hiredate,d.dname
FROM emp e, dept d
where e.deptno= d.deptno
```

and d.deptno = :P15_DEPT
ORDER by ename

Step 10: Then, Navigate to Layout section and select "Start New Row" as **No.**

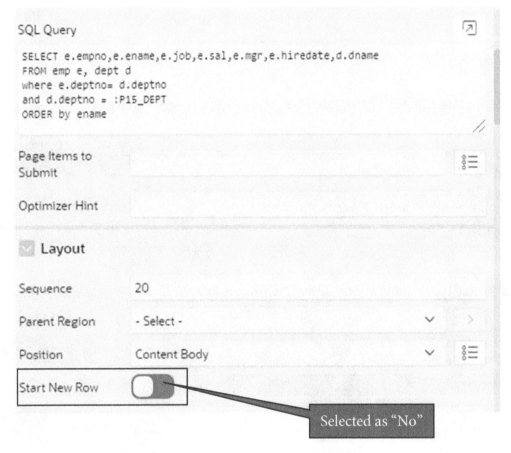

Selected as "No"

Step 11: Create a Dynamic action as follows.

Event :**Click**

Selection Type :**jQuery Selector**

jQuery Selector :**.cList-dept**

Step 12: Create three True Action as follows.

True Action 1

Action: **Execute JavaScript code**

#Sample Code

```
//replace P15_DEPT with your page item
var dept_id = $('#P15_DEPT').val();
if (dept_id != "") {
    $("#" + dept_id).removeClass("cSelected");
}
apex.item("P15_DEPT").setValue(this.triggeringElement.id);
$("#" + this.triggeringElement.id).addClass("cSelected");
```

True Action 2

Action : **Execute Javascript code**

PL/SQLCode : **Null**

Items to Submit : **P15_DEPT(Hidden field)** //replace P15_DEPTwith your page item

True Action 3

Action : **Refresh**

Selection Type : **Region**

Region : **Employee Report**(Classic Report)

Step 13: Save and Run the page.

Output:

The final screen will look like a picture as shown below. By clicking on the Department in the list view will refresh the Employee Report (Classic Report) and display the employee data for the selected Department without page submission.

Source : https://krutten.blogspot.com/2018/06/46-list-view-in-apex-181.html

5.1.9 PL/SQL Dynamic Content

Introduction to PL/SQL Dynamic Content

PL/SQL Dynamic Content region is based on PL/SQ. It enables to render any HTML or text using the PL/SQL Web Util Packages.

Use case for PL/SQL Dynamic Content

5.1.9.1 Requirement:

Let's try to create a Student's Report card using PL/SQL Dynamic Content.

Solution:

Step1: Create a Blank Page

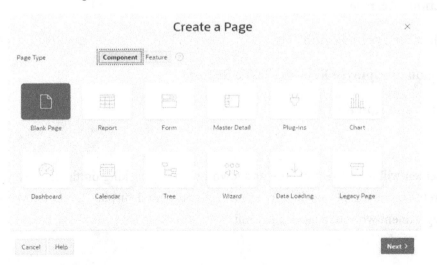

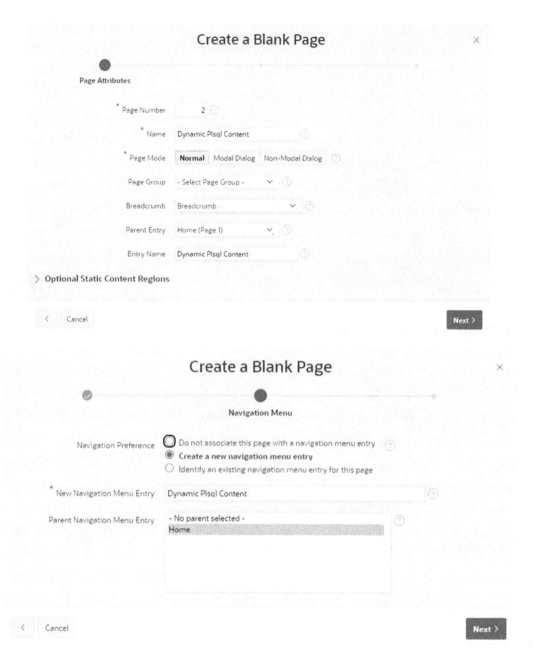

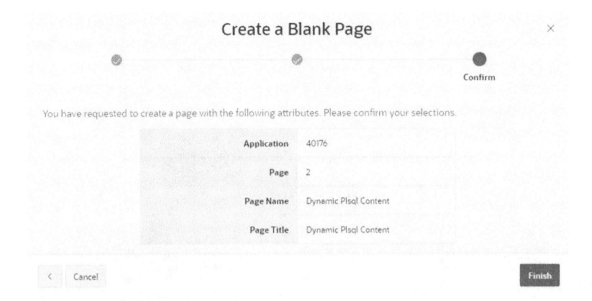

Step 2: Create a static content Region.

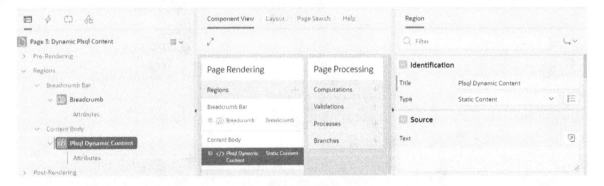

Step 3: Assign the Region type as PL/SQL Dynamic Content.

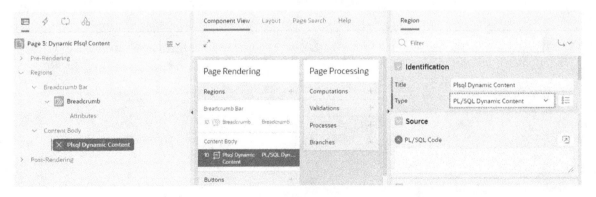

Step 4: Enter the below code in the *Source*.

#Sample Code

```
BEGIN
  FOR X IN (SELECT ROWID
,SID
,STUDENT_NAME
,STUDENT_ROLL_NUMBER
,STUDENT_DOB
,STUDENT_AGE
,GRADE
,RESULT
,SCHEDULE_DATE
        FROM STUDENT_MASTER
        WHERE STUDENT_NAME = :P9_STUDENT_NAME) LOOP
   HTP.P
     ('<style type="text/css">
.ab1 table tr td{font-size:14px;
                    border-top:5px solid  BOLD;
                   border-bottom: 2px solid  BOLD;
border-collapse:collapse;
                   }
.ab11 table tr td{font-size:14px;
                   border-right: 2px solid  BLACK;
border-collapse:collapse;
                   margin:0px 0px 0px0px;
                   }
.Doyen{float:left;
border:{border-style: dotted;};
    height:3.2IN;
    font-size:16px; }
.Doyen{float:left;
 border: 21px solid transparent;
  padding: 15px;
  -webkit-border-image: url(#APP_IMAGES#Goldenborder.png) 30 round; /* Safari 3.1-
5 */
```

```
    -o-border-image: url(#APP_IMAGES#Goldenborder.png    ) 30 round; /* Opera 11-12.1
*/
    border-image: url(#APP_IMAGES#Goldenborder.png    ) 30 round;
}
}
.Doyen table {    width: 100%;
height:auto;
            border:1 px solid black;
        }
.Doyen table  tr{width: 100%;
height:auto;
            padding:6px 6px 6px6px;
        }
.Doyen table  tr td{width: ;
            height:10px;
font:verdana;
border-collapse:collapse;
            padding:8px 8px 8px8px;
            font-size:16px;
        }
.form_b{border-right:none;
border-left:none;
border-top:none;
border-bottom:dotted #000 2px;
  WIDTH:890PX;
}
.ab2 table {    width: 100%;
height:auto;
            border:1 px solid black;
        }
.ab2 table  tr{width: 100%;
height:auto;
            padding:6px 6px 6px6px;
        }
.ab2 table  tr td{width: ;
            height:5px;
```

```
font:verdana;
            font-size:16px;
          }
</style> '
    );
   HTP.P (' <div  class="Doyen"> ');
   HTP.P (' <table> ');
   HTP.P  ('<span   style="font-size:15px;   color:bold;"><center><b><otsl></otsl>Student
Reports Card</B></CENTER> ');
   HTP.P     ('<span    style="font-size:15px;    color:bold;"><center><b><otsl>Chennai,
India</otsl></B></CENTER> ');
   HTP.P (   '<tr><td STYLE="width=15%;">Student Name </td><td WIDTH=1%>:</td><td
class="form_b"  STYLE="WIDTH:400PX;">'
       || HTF.ESCAPE_SC (X.STUDENT_NAME)
       || '</td><td  width=15%>  Student  Roll  No  </td><td  WIDTH=1%>:</td><td
class="form_b">'
       || HTF.ESCAPE_SC (X.SID)
       || '</td>'
       );
   HTP.P  ('<tr><td   width=15%>  Student  Grade  </td><td  WIDTH=1%>:</td><td
class="form_b">' || HTF.ESCAPE_SC (X.GRADE) || '</td><tr></tr>');
   HTP.P (      '<tr><tr><td width=15%> Student Age </td><td WIDTH=1%>:</td><td
class="form_b">'
       || HTF.ESCAPE_SC (X.STUDENT_AGE)
       || '</td>
<td width=15%>Result </td><td WIDTH=1%>:</td><td class="form_b">'
       || HTF.ESCAPE_SC (X.RESULT)
       || '</td></tr>'
       );
   HTP.P ('</table> ');
   HTP.P ('<br>');
   HTP.P ('</table> ');
  END LOOP;
END;
```

Output:

Student Report Card will appear as below:

5.1.10 Region Display Selector

Introduction to Region Display Selector

The Region Display Selector is a Region's component that provides a page level navigation control for other regions with the *Region Display Selector* property set to *Yes*. It can be configured to work in two modes:

- **View Single Region** Show regions as tabs. Selecting a tab will make the corresponding region visible and hide the other selections.
- **Scroll Window** Always display all the regions on the page. Selecting a tab will scroll your window to the corresponding region.

Use Case for Region Display selector

5.1.10.1   Requirement 1:

Let's see how to dynamically toggle between the tables in Region Display selector.

Step 1: Create Main region and add the Sub regions and assign static Ids to both the regions.

Step 2: Create Page item by which we can assign value to display the region.

Step 3: Createprocess where we assign value to the Page item.

#Sample Code

```
BEGIN
    IF :P21_SWITCH_REGION = '1' THEN
            :P21_SWITCH_REGION := '2';
    ELSIF :P21_SWITCH_REGION = '2' THEN
            :P21_SWITCH_REGION := '1';
    END IF;
END;
```

Step 4: Place the JavaScript in *'Function and Global Variable Declaration'*.

#Sample Code

```
$(window).bind("load", function() {
setTimeout(function() {
tab_click();
   }, 1000);
});

function tab_click() {
   if ($('#P21_SWITCH_REGION').val() == '1') {
     $("#SR_REGION1_tab > a").click();
   }
   if ($('#P21_SWITCH_REGION').val() == '2') {
     $("#SR_REGION2_tab > a").click();
   }
}
```

Output:

On page submit based on the page item value it will toggle between regions.

5.1.10.2 *Requirement 2:*

We need to freeze the Region items, Buttons and Region Display Selector Region at the top when we Scroll down to bottom.

Solution:

You could achieve this by adding JavaScript and CSS in the APEX page. Let us see the step by step process to achieve this.

Step 1: Create two or more Region then change the first region type into Regional Display Selector.After that add the other regions into region display selector by changing 'Yes' in the Regional Display Selector option in the Region Level Setting(Advance).

Step 2: Create another region with static region type. Change the sequence to 1. Create the button (Cancel, Create, Delete, Apply Changes) and Item (item which needs to display on all tabs) in this region.

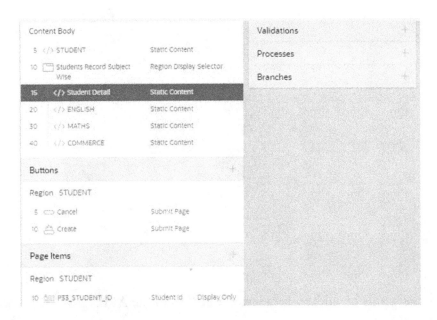

Step 3: Add static id 'TEST' into the static region, which is created at the step 2.

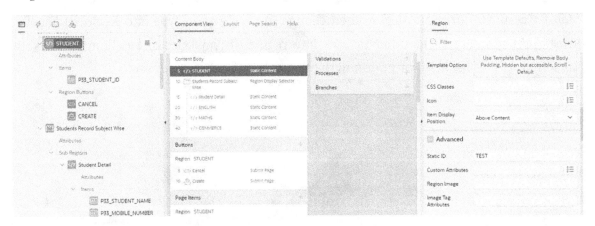

Step 4: Add the below code into the JavaScript on page load.

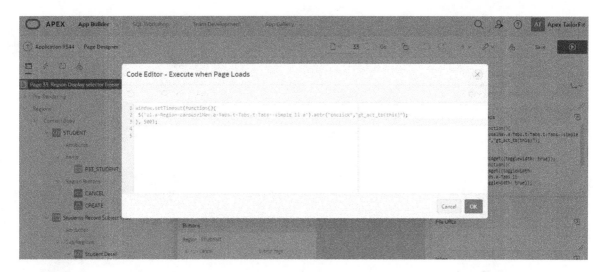

#*Sample Code*

```
window.setTimeout(function(){
 $('#TEST').stickyWidget({toggleWidth: true})&&$('ul.a-Region-carouselNav.a-Tabs.t-
Tabs.t-Tabs--simple li a').stickyWidget({toggleWidth: true});
 }, 500);
```

Use this code in APEX 20.

#*Sample Code*

```
window.setTimeout(function(){
 $('#TEST').stickyWidget({toggleWidth: true})&&$('ul.apex-rds.a-Tabs li
a').stickyWidget({toggleWidth: true});
 }, 500);
```

If You want to Change the color use the Below step.

Step 5:Add below code in Inline CSS,

#*Sample Code*

```
.t-Region-body{
   background-color: #e7e7e7 !important;
}
```

Output:

5.1.11 Static Content

Introduction to Static Content

One of the significant region components in Oracle APEX region is Static Content. As the name denotes, the Static Content has no dynamicity or perform any operation. But it's more like a prime white canvas for a painter and it's up to our imagination to do wonders with HTML, CSS and JavaScript.

LearningObjective

The static content renders the content entered in the "*Source*"attribute as HTML so we can display the same in the application. Since it is like a white canvas, we can build a customized solution using this functionality of static content. Below is a use case for Static Content:

Use case for Static Content:

5.1.11.1   *Requirement:*

Let us dynamically create a merged row for a specific column when a row is added similar to a merge row functionality in Excel, refer to samples.

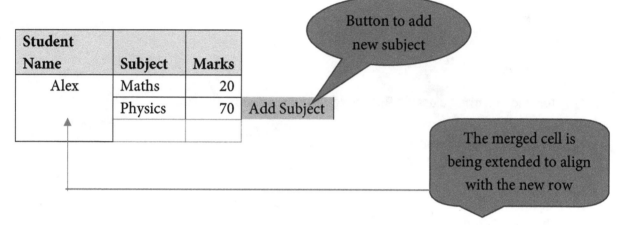

Student Name	Subject	Marks
	Maths	20
Alex	Physics	70

Add Subject

On click of **Add Subject** button a new row has been added to capture the subject and marks for the student Alex.

Button to add new subject

Student Name	Subject	Marks
Alex	Maths	20
	Physics	70

Add Subject

The merged cell is being extended to align with the new row

Solution:

You could achieve this using HTML and JavaScript in Oracle APEX static region. Let us see the step by step process to achieve this.

Step 1: Create a HTML heading for the table.

Student Name	Student Subject	Student Mark

In the Region "*Source*", add the below code as displayed in the screenshot:

```
Source

Text                                                    ⌐⌐

<table id="myhtml" class="t-Report-report" style="width:100%">
    <tr>
        <th class="t-Report-colHead" id="STU_ID_HID" style="display: none">Student
ID Hidden</th>
        <th class="t-Report-colHead" id="STU_NAME">Student Name</th>
        <th class="t-Report-colHead" id="STU_SUB" >Student Subject</th>
        <th class="t-Report-colHead" id="STU_MARK" >Student Mark</th>
        <th class="edit" style="border-left: 1px solid #00433c;width: 25px"
id="MARK_DEL"></th>

    </tr>
```

#Sample Code

```
<table id="myhtml" class="t-Report-report" style="width:100%">
<tr>
<th class="t-Report-colHead" id="STU_ID_HID" style="display:
        none">Student ID Hidden</th>
<th class="t-Report-colHead" id="STU_NAME">Student Name</th>
<th class="t-Report-colHead" id="STU_SUB" >Student Subject</th>
<th class="t-Report-colHead" id="STU_MARK" >Student Mark</th>
<th class="edit" style="border-left: 1px solid #00433c;width: 25px"
        id="MARK_DEL"></th>
</tr>
</table>
```

To achieve the styles, add the below CSS.

```
<style>
.t-Report-colHead
{
    background-color:#0076df;
    color: #FFFFFF;
}
</style>
<table id="myhtml" class="t-Report-report" style="width:100%">
    ...........
</table>
```

Step 2: Creating a merged row when the button "**Add Subject**" is pressed using a JavaScript function "**addSubject()**".

```
<style>
...
</style>
<table id="myhtml" class="t-Report-report" style="width:100%">
...
</table>
<div>
<span class="edit" id="insnewstu" onclick="addStudent()" style="margin-left:
45px;">Insert New Student</span>
</div>
```

On the "*Function and Global Variable Declaration*" of the page, type in the below JavaScript function code.

#Sample Code

// To add rows in the HTML region, add the below JavaScript code

```
function addStudent()
{
```

```
$('#ADD_MARK').remove();
var last_row_index = $('#myhtmltr:last').index();
max_row += 1;
var add_mark = '<div><br><input type="button" class="addmark" id="ADD_MARK"
    onclick="add_mark(this)" value="Add Subject"></div>';
var row = "<tr id=row_" + max_row + ">" +

"<td class='myhtmltd1' id='f13_" + max_row + "' headers='STU_ID'
    style='display: none'><input type='text'></td>" +
"<td class='myhtmltd' id='f10_" + max_row + "' headers='STU_ID_HID'
    style='display: none'><input type='text' id=stu_id_hid" + max_row + "></td>" +
"<td class='myhtmltd' id='f02_" + max_row + "' headers='STU_NAME'><textarea
class='myhtmlitem text apex-item-textarea' maxlength='200' type='text'
class='text_field apex-item-text'></textarea></td>" +
"<td class='myhtmltd' id='f04_" + max_row + "' headers='STU_SUB'><textarea
class='myhtmlitem text apex-item-textarea' maxlength='200' type='text'
class='text_field apex-item-text'></textarea>" + add_mark + "</td>" +
"<td class='myhtmltd' id='f06_" + max_row + "' headers='MARK'><textarea
class='myhtmlitem text apex-item-textarea' maxlength='200' type='text'
class='text_field apex-item-text'></textarea></td>" +
 "</tr>";

if ($('#myhtml>tbody> tr').length> 1)
 {
  var newid = $('#myhtmltr:last').prop('id');
  $("#" + newid).after(row);
 }
else if ($('#myhtml>tbody> tr').length == 1)
 {
  $("#myhtml").append(row);
 }
 }

// To Add Subjects and mark, include the below code

function add_mark(addrow)
 {
```

```
var curr_td_element = $(addrow).parents('td')
var first_rw_no = $(curr_td_element).parents('tr').index();

if (true)
 {
    var rowspan = $(curr_td_element).prop("rowspan");
    var row_num = $(addrow).parents('tr').index();
    var row_id = $(addrow).parents('tr').prop('id');
      $('#ADD_MARK').remove();
      var add_mark = '<div><br><input type="button" class="addmark"
        id="ADD_MARK" onclick="add_mark(this)" value="Add Subject"></div>';
max_row += 1;
      var new_error = "<tr id=row_" + max_row + ">" +
        "<td class='myhtmltd' id='f04_" + max_row + "'
          headers='STU_SUB'><textarea class='myhtmlitem text apex-item-
textarea' maxlength='200' type='text' class='text_field apex-item-
          text'></textarea>" + add_mark + "</td>" +
        "<td class='myhtmltd' id='f06_" + max_row + "'
          headers='MARK'><textarea class='myhtmlitem text apex-item-
textarea' maxlength='200' type='text' class='text_field apex-item-
          text'></textarea></td>" +
        "</tr>";
      $('#' + row_id).after(new_error);
      var flg = 'N';
      $('#myhtml>tbody>tr:nth-child(' + parseInt(first_rw_no + 1) +
        ')').find('td').each(function()
       {
        var header = $(this).attr('headers');
        if (header == "STU_NAME") {
            $('#P1_NEW').val($(this).attr('id'));
flg = 'Y';
            $(this).prop('rowspan', parseInt(rowspan + 1));
        }
      });
      if (flg == 'N')
       {
```

```
        var rw_id = $('#P1_NEW').val();
        var rw_s = parseInt($('#' + rw_id).prop('rowspan')) + 1;
        $('#' + rw_id).prop('rowspan', rw_s);
     }
   }
 }
```

Output:

Now UI of the merged row is as follows:

5.1.12 Tree

Introduction to Tree

Tree is an Oracle APEX component which creates the hierarchical view based on a query.

Oracle APEX Tree was introduced from release 5.0. This feature, like legacy jsTree region and isbased on JavaScript, cross browser component with optional keyboard navigation and state saving.

Tree can be created from a query based on a hierarchical relationship identified by ID and parent ID column, using start with and connect by clause. Tree can also be created using the "Create Page Wizard", which generates this hierarchical query based on the options selected.

Use case for Tree

5.1.12.1 Requirement:

Let's give some extra touch to a tree where we try to create a checkbox to each node of the tree and we can get the value of the selected node from the checkbox.

Solution:

This could be achieved using JavaScript. This customization works only with Version 5.0. Let us see the step by step process to achieve this.

Step1: Create tree region with the following script.

#Sample Code

```
SELECT   CASE
         WHEN CONNECT_BY_ISLEAF = 1
           THEN 0
         WHEN LEVEL = 1
           THEN 1
```

```
        ELSE -1
      END AS status,
      LEVEL, STUDENT_NAME AS title, NULL AS icon,
      SID AS VALUE, GRADE AS tooltip, NULL AS LINK
    FROM student_master
 START WITH incharge is null
CONNECT BY PRIOR SID = incharge
 ORDER SIBLINGS BY SID;
```

Step2: Create Page item **P81_LIST_ID**.

Step3: Place this JavaScript in the page header.

#Sample Code

```javascript
regTree = apex.jQuery("#Treestatic-id").find("div.tree");
regTree.tree({
ui: {
theme_name: "checkbox"
  },
  callback: {
onchange: function(NODE, TREE_OBJ) {
        if (TREE_OBJ.settings.ui.theme_name == "checkbox") {
          var $this = $(NODE).is("li") ? $(NODE) : $(NODE).parent();
          if ($this.children("a.unchecked").size() == 0) {
TREE_OBJ.container.find("a").addClass("unchecked");
          }
          $this.children("a").removeClass("clicked");
          if ($this.children("a").hasClass("checked")) {

$this.find("li").andSelf().children("a").removeClass("checked").removeClass("undetermined").addClass("unchecked");
            var state = 0;
          } else {

$this.find("li").andSelf().children("a").removeClass("unchecked").removeClass("undetermined").addClass("checked");
```

106

```
                var state = 1;
            }
        $this.parents("li").each(function() {
            if (state == 1) {
                if    ($(this).find("a.unchecked,    a.undetermined").size()    -    1    >    0)    {
$(this).parents("li").andSelf().children("a").removeClass("unchecked").removeClass("check
ed").addClass("undetermined");
                    return false;
                }                                                                  else
$(this).children("a").removeClass("unchecked").removeClass("undetermined").addClass("ch
ecked");
            } else {
                if    ($(this).find("a.checked,    a.undetermined").size()    -    1    >    0)    {
$(this).parents("li").andSelf().children("a").removeClass("unchecked").removeClass("check
ed").addClass("undetermined");
                    return false;
                }                                                                  else
$(this).children("a").removeClass("checked").removeClass("undetermined").addClass("unch
ecked");
            }});
        }},
onopen: function(NODE, TREE_OBJ) {
        $(NODE).removeClass("open").addClass("closed");
    },
onclose: function(NODE, TREE_OBJ) {
        $(NODE).removeClass("closed").addClass("open");
    }}});
document.getElementById("tree373743011093796525").onclick = function() {
clickFunction()
};

function clickFunction() {
    var lPassengers = [];
    $(".leafa.checked").parent()
.each(function() {
lPassengers.push($(this).attr("id"))
```

107

```
    });
  $s("P81_LIST_ID", lPassengers.join(":"));
}


$(document).ready(function() {
$.each($v("P81_LIST_ID").split(":"),
function(intIndex, objValue) {
        $("li#" + objValue + ".leaf a:first-child").click();
    });
});
```

Output:

The Screen would appear as below:

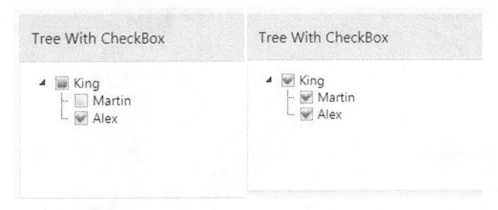

5.1.13 Date Picker

Introduction to Date Picker

The Date picker is an Item component in Oracle APEX Page Item. This item displays a text field along with a Calendar icon. The User could either enter the date or select using the Calendar icon. Time is optional and it is displayed if the Format Mask for this item includes time components.

Learning Objective

Standard Date picker displays the calendar in the format shown below. Using JavaScript in Dynamic actions, we can develop a few other display features in Date Picker. Let us explore using a few sample cases.

Standard Date Picker

Use case for Date Picker:

5.1.13.1 Requirement 1

To display the first day of the week as Monday instead of Sunday.

Solution:

You could achieve this using Execute JavaScript in Dynamic Actions. Let us see the step by step process to achieve this.

Step 1: Create a *Page* item and set as Type "*Date Picker*".

Place the help text values in *Help -> InlineHelp Text.*

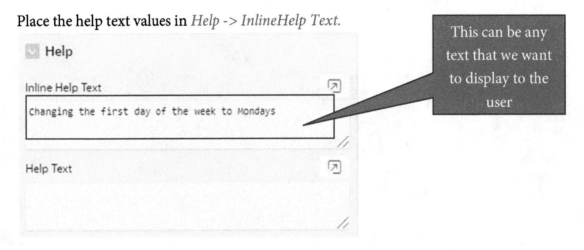

This can be any text that we want to display to the user

Step2: Create a *Dynamic action* and set *when Event* condition as "*Page Load*".

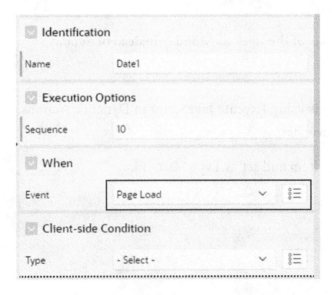

Set the "*True Action*" as *Execute JavaScript Code* and set the Item under *Affected Elements*.

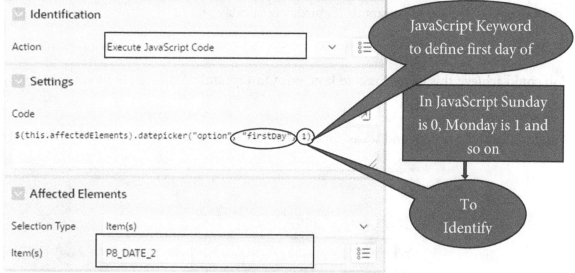

#*Sample Code:*

```
$(this.affectedElements).datepicker("option", "firstDay", 1);
$(this.affectedElements).next('button').addClass('a-Button a-Button--calendar');
```

Output:

Now UI of the Date Picker is as follows with first day of the week as Monday:

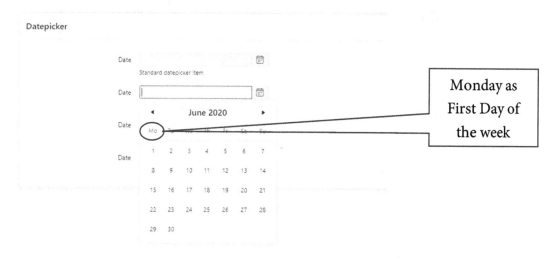

5.1.13.2 Requirement 2

To disable the selection of weekends (Saturday & Sunday).

Solution:

You could achieve this using Execute JavaScript in Dynamic Actions. Let us see the step by step process to achieve this.

Step 1: Create a *Page* item and set as Type "*Date Picker*".

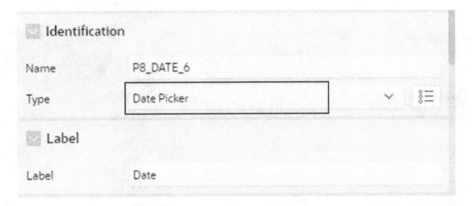

Place the help text values in *Help -> InlineHelp Text.*

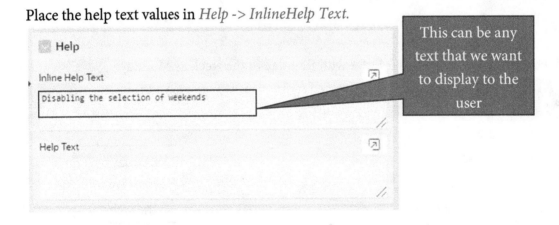

Step2: Create a *Dynamic action* and set *when Event* condition as "*Page Load*".

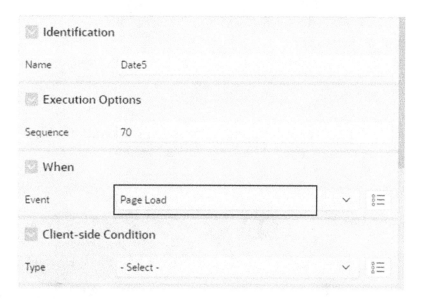

Set the "*True Action*" as *Execute JavaScript Code* and set the Item under *Affected Elements*.

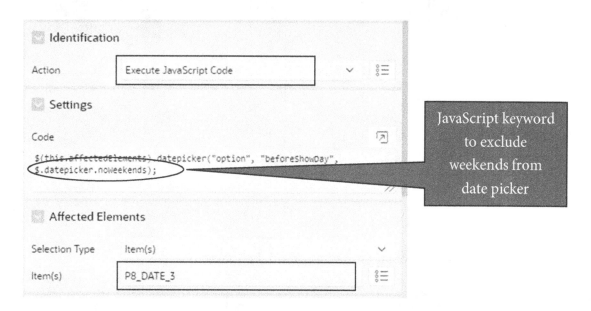

#Sample Code:

```
$(this.affectedElements).datepicker("option", "beforeShowDay",
$.datepicker.noWeekends);
$(this.affectedElements).next('button').addClass('a-Button a-Button--calendar');
```

Output:

Now UI of the Date Picker is as follows with selection of weekends disabled:

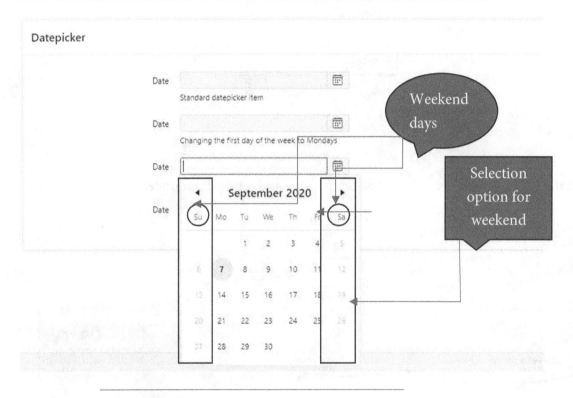

5.1.13.3 Requirement 3:

To disable the selection of days other than weekend. Eg. Monday.

Solution:

You could achieve this using Execute JavaScript in Dynamic Actions. Let us see the step by step process to achieve this.

Step 1: Create a *Page* item and set as Type "*Date Picker*".

Identification

Name	P8_DATE_4
Type	Date Picker

Label

Label	Date

Place the help text values in *Help -> InlineHelp Text.*

Help

Inline Help Text

Disabling the selection of Mondays

Help Text

> This can be any text that we want to display to the user

Step2: Place the Javascript Function in Page *Function and Global Variable Declaration* section.

Function and Global Variable Declaration

```
function disableMondays(pDate){
    var lTooltipDate = "Tooltip for disabled dates";
    if (pDate.getDay() === 1){
        return [false, 'disabledDayClass', lTooltipDate];
    }
    else {
        return [true, null, null];
    }
}
```

> In JavaScript Sunday is 0, Monday is 1 and so on

> To Identify Monday

#Sample Code:

```
function disableMondays(pDate){
    var lTooltipDate = "Tooltip for disabled dates";
    if (pDate.getDay() === 1) {
        return [false, 'disabledDayClass', lTooltipDate];
    }
    else {
        return [true, null, null];
    }
}
```

Step3: Create a *Dynamic action* and set *when Event* condition as *"Page Load"*.

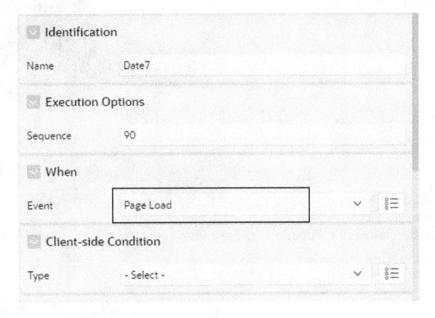

Set the *"True Action"* as *Execute JavaScript Code* and set the Item under *Affected Elements*.

#*Sample Code:*

$(this.affectedElements).datepicker("option", "beforeShowDay", function(date) {return disableMondays(date);});

$(this.affectedElements).next('button').addClass('a-Button a-Button--calendar');

Output:

Now UI of the Date Picker is as follows with selection of Monday disabled:

Disabling the selection of Mondays

5.2 ITEMS

An item is part of an HTML form. An item can be a text field, text area, password, select list, check box and so on. Item attributes impacts the display of Item in a page. Developers can control how a page item works by editing the page item attributes. The following table describes key attributes that control item functionality.

5.2.1 Checkbox

Introduction to Check box

A checkbox is an input option that represents a setting or value with an on, off or mixed choice. A check mark within the checkbox indicates that the setting is selected or checked.

Checkboxes in a group are non-exclusive options; more than one checkbox in a group can be checked at any given time.

Learning Objective

Creating check box is relatively easy. By default, the Oracle APEX allows creating a simple check box in the HTML region. The HTML region types are used for forms in Oracle APEX.

Use case for Check box:

5.2.1.1 Requirement:

By default, the check box is shown as a ticked (checked) square box when activated. But it can be modified to any other symbol.

Solution:

You could achieve this by adding minimal CSS in Oracle APEX. Let us see the step by step process to achieve this:

Step 1:Create a region in the name **Check Box** and select region type as Static Content.

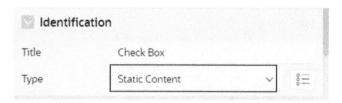

Step 2: Create a Check Box and name it as Regular Check Box.

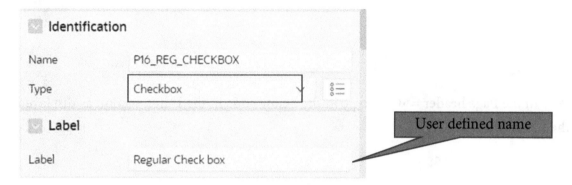

Step 3: Create another Check Box and name it as Customized Check Box.

Step 4: Go to Advance section of **Customized Check box**(P16_CUST_CHECKBOX) and add a text **fancy-checkbox** to CSS classes attribute as shown in the below screen shot.

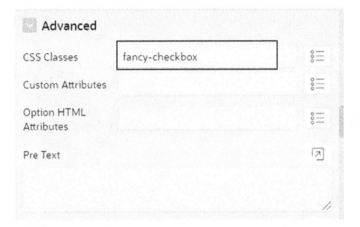

Step 5: In the Page header =>CSS, type in the below code in the Inline section as displayed in the screen shot.

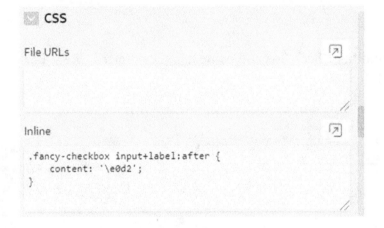

#Sample Code

```
.fancy-checkbox input+label:after {
    content: '\e0d2';
}
```

Step 6: Finally, Save and Run the page.

Output:

Below screen shot shows the difference in the style of the Regular Check box and Customized Check box.

Check Box

5.2.2 File Browse

Introduction to File Browse

The "File Browse" item shows a text field with the browse button. The browse button allows the user to locate and upload the file from a local file system.

While creating a "File Browse" item, if the "Storage Type" option is selected as "Table APEX_APPLICATION_TEMP_FILES", then it stores the uploaded file(s) in a temporary location which we can access using the VIEW APEX_APPLICATION_TEMP_FILES. The "File Browse "item will not support for Interactive Grid columns.

The "File Browse" Item storage type includes two types:

- BLOB column specified in Item Source attribute
- Table APEX_APPLICATION_TEMP_FILES

BLOB column specified in Item Source attribute:

The BLOB column specified in the Item Source attribute will store the uploaded file in the Automatic Row Processing (DML) process and the column specified in the Source attribute of the object.

Table APEX_APPLICATION_TEMP_FILES:

It saves the uploaded file(s) to a temporary location that can be accessed using the VIEW APEX_APPLICATION_TEMP_FILES. APEX can delete the file(s) automatically at the end of the session or at the end of the request for upload, depending up on the settings value of the attribute "**Purge File At**".

Learning Objective

The "File Upload" feature has a significant update from APEX 5.1 version, thus we can also allow users to pick multiple files (from a single directory) at the same time by merely changing attributes on the object shown in the below screen shot.

Additionally, you can now limit the type of file that user can select, based on the file's MIME type, e.g. image/jpg. Such limitation of the form of the file may use a wildcard, e.g. image/ * and may have several patterns separated by commas, e.g. image/png, application/pdf.

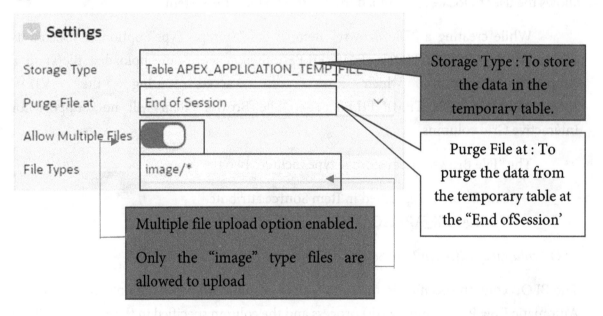

Use case for File Browse:

5.2.2.1   Requirement:

By default, the file browse is shown as a text field with a browse button. But it can be modified to different look and feel. Let us have the requirement on how to change a style of simple file browse item to Drag and Drop look and feel.

Solution:

We can achieve this by adding minimal CSS and JavaScript in Oracle APEX. Let us see the step by step process to achieve this.

Step 1: Create a region in the name **File Browse** and select region type as Static Content.

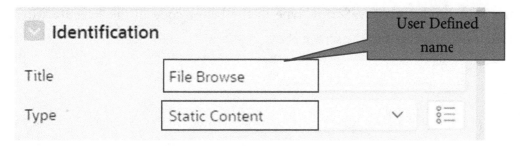

Step 2: Create an item File Browse and name it as Regular File Browse.

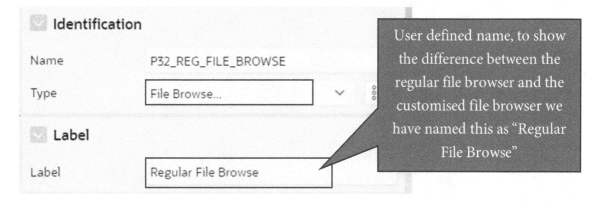

Step 3: Create one more item File Browse and name it as Customized File Browse.

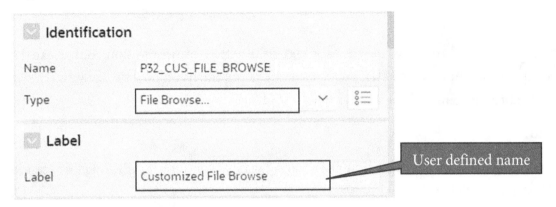

Step 4: In the Page header ==>**JavaScript**, type in the below code in the **Execute when Page Loads** section as displayed in the screen shot.

#*Sample Code*

```
//replace P32_CUS_FILE_BROWSE with your page item
$( "#P32_CUS_FILE_BROWSE" ).parent().addClass("item-group");
$( "#P32_CUS_FILE_BROWSE" ).next().addClass("item-dropzone");
```

```
$( ".item-dropzone .apex-item-file-dropzone-label" ).text('Drag your files here or click in this area');
```

Step 5: Navigate to CSS section and add the below code in the "Inline" attribute as shown in the below screen shot.

#Sample Code

```
.item-group{
position: relative;
    font-size: 18px;
    width: 100%;
    padding: 50px 30px !important;
    border: 2px dashed #ccc;
    background-color: #fff;
    text-align: center;
    transition: background 0.3s ease-in-out;
}
//replace P32_CUS_FILE_BROWSE with your page item
#P32_CUS_FILE_BROWSE {
                position: absolute;
```

```
        height: 100%;
        top: 0;
        left: 0;
        right: 0;
        bottom: 0;
        opacity: 0;
        cursor: pointer;
    }
    .item-dropzone {
        position: inherit !important;
    }
    .item-dropzone .apex-item-file-dropzone-label{
    border-style:hidden !important;
    }
    .item-dropzone .apex-item-file-dropzone-icon {
    display:none;
    }
```

Step 6: Finally, Save and Run the page.

Output: Below screen shot shows the difference in the style of the Regular File Browse and Customized File Browse.

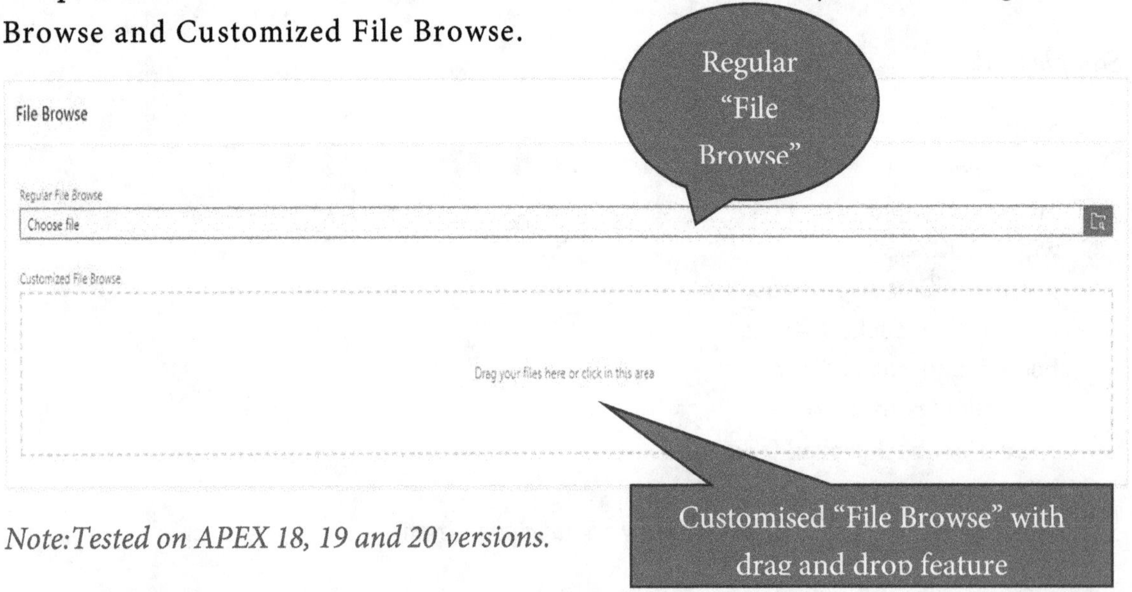

Note: Tested on APEX 18, 19 and 20 versions.

5.2.3 List Manager

Introduction to List Manager

List Manager is an item type, that allows users to enter values and it will be added in the list. It displays as a text item with a popup list of values icons, Add and Remove buttons and a list of selected values. User can type in the value or pick from the list of available items. User can then utilize the buttons to manage the values selected.

Learning Objective

List Manager allows users to add or remove multiple values. Shuttle and list manager are handling mostly same feature. If the list of value is very high, then we go for the list Manager. Below is the use case for list manager.

Use case for List Manager:

5.2.3.1 Requirement:

Let us consider the List Manager holds the list of employees, the details of the selected employees should be displayed in the Interactive report.

Employee List Manager
7499-ALLEN
7782-CLARK
7839-KING

Here the selected value is "King", then the report will show the Employee "King" details. If user selected multiple values, the selected employee details will be displayed as report.

Solution:

Step 1: Create a Region Employees as Static Content.

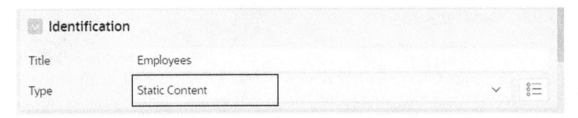

Step 2: Create a new item for List Manager, under the region "Employees".

In List of Values, select type as "SQL Query" and place the below code.

#Sample Code

```
select enamed,empno||'-'||ename r from emp;
```

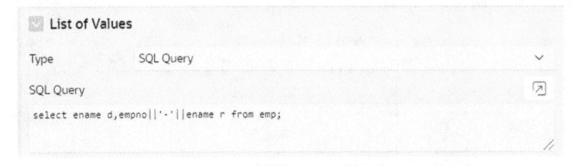

Step 3: Create a new text field, to hold the selected values in the List Manager.

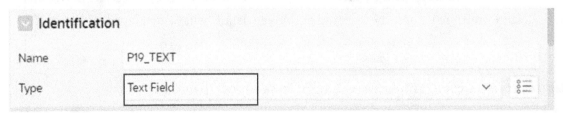

Step 4: Create a new Interactive Report, with title as Employee Details.Place the below code in the Source SQL Type:

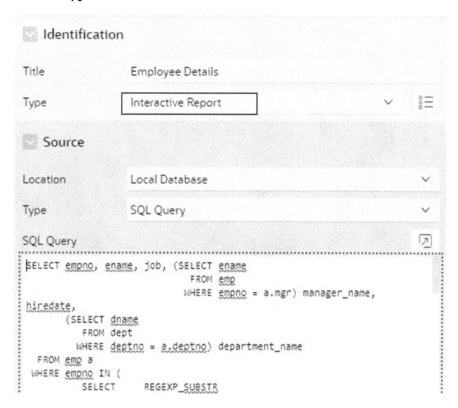

#Sample Code

```
SELECT empno, ename, job, (SELECT ename
                FROM emp
                WHERE empno = a.mgr) manager_name, hiredate,
     (SELECT dname
       FROM dept
      WHERE deptno = a.deptno) department_name
   FROM emp a
  WHERE empno IN (
      SELECT    REGEXP_SUBSTR
             ((SELECT REGEXP_REPLACE ((REGEXP_REPLACE (:p19_text,
                                   '[^0-9]+',
                                   ' ',
```

```
                                )
                            ),
                            ',$',
                            ''

                        )
                FROM DUAL),
            '[^,]+',
            1,
            LEVEL
            )
        FROM DUAL
    CONNECT BY REGEXP_SUBSTR
            ((SELECT REGEXP_REPLACE ((REGEXP_REPLACE (:p19_text,
                            '[^0-9]+',
                            ' ',
                            )

                            ),
                            ',$',
                            ''

                        )
                FROM DUAL),
            '[^,]+',
            1,
            LEVEL
            ) IS NOT NULL)
```

*Step 5:*Create a new Dynamic Action, to get the selected values in List Manager and place the output value in "P19_TEXT".

Event: Click

Selection Type: Items

Items: P19_EMPLOYEE

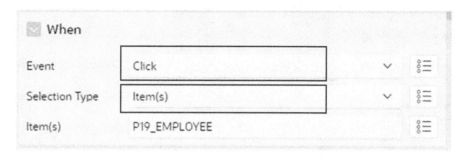

Step 6: Create a True Action Process.

Process 1:

Action: Execute JavaScript Code

Place the below script in code editor.

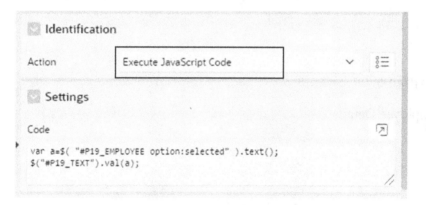

#Sample Code

```
var a=$( "#P19_EMPLOYEE option:selected" ).text();
$("#P19_TEXT").val(a);
```

Process 2:

Action: Execute PL/SQL Code

In PL/SQL Code, set the value as "NULL".

Items to Submit: P19_TEXT

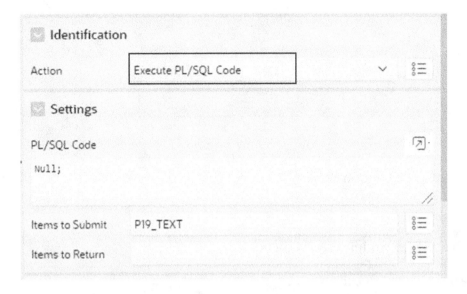

Process 3:

Action: Refresh

SelectionType: Region

Region: Employee Details

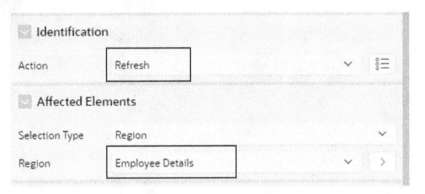

Click Save and Run the Page.

Output:

Selected Employee: ALLEN

Selecting Multiple Employees:

Employee Selected: Clark, King

Two employees selected in the list

Selected employee details displayed in the report

5.2.4 Number Field

Introduction to Number Field

Number Field is an item type to display Numbers. This item automatically validates the entered value and ensure it's a number. No additional manual validations are required. Also, by configuring the Minimum Value and Maximum Value attributes of Number field item, we could predefine the allowed number range validation for values entered.

Learning Objective

Since Number field is like a text box, it also allows entering any special characters, numbers or alphabets. Only at the time of page submission we get the error message, if any values other than number is entered in this field. So, we can build a customized solution to restrict entering Non-Numeric Characters in the Number field. Below is the use case for Number field.

Use case for Number field:

5.2.4.1 Requirement

In this use case, Marks Column is a Number field with Mark range as 35 to 100, whenever user tries to enter a Non-Numeric Character an alert should be displayed.

Minimum Range: 35

Maximum Range: 100

Student Name	Alex
Subject	Maths
Marks	70

Solution:

You could achieve this using JavaScript. Let us see the step by step process to achieve the above requirement.

Step 1: Create a New Items as Student name, Subject, Marks. For Student name, Subject set the type as "Text Field". For Marks Column set as Number Field.

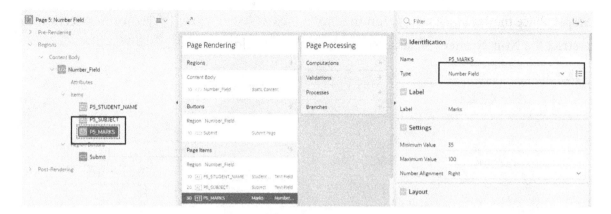

Step 2:Minimum Value - Enter the minimum value permitted.

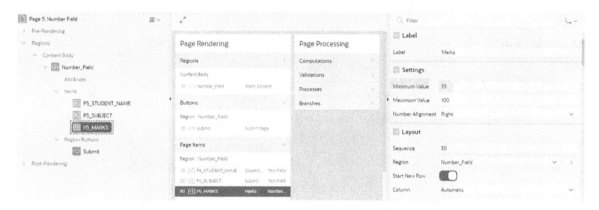

Step 3: Maximum Value - Enter the maximum value permitted.

Step 4: Place the JavaScript Function in *Function and Global Variable Declaration* section to restrict the Non-Numeric Characters in the Number field.

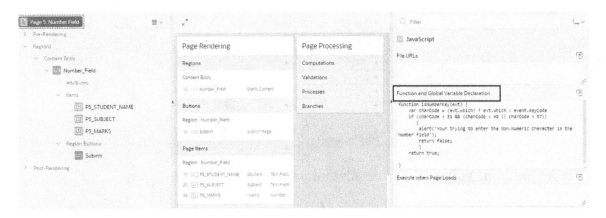

#*Sample Code:*

```
function isNumberKey(evt) {
    var charCode = (evt.which) ? evt.which : event.keyCode
    if (charCode> 31 && (charCode< 48 || charCode> 57))
        return false;
    return true;
}
```

Step 5: Call the function **isNumberKey()onkeypress** event of the Marks Column. Add the code in the *Advanced -> Custom Attributes* Section.

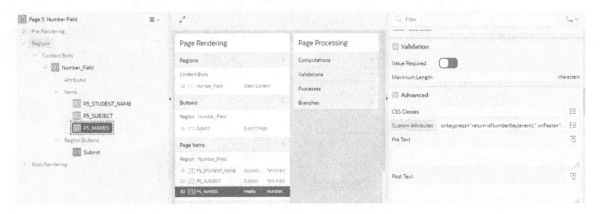

#Sample Code

```
onkeypress="return isNumberKey(event);" onPaste="return false"
```

Output:

Enter the value for Mark as Non-Numeric Character as "A".

The alert message will be displayed as below. User can't enter the Non-Numeric Characters in Marks Field.

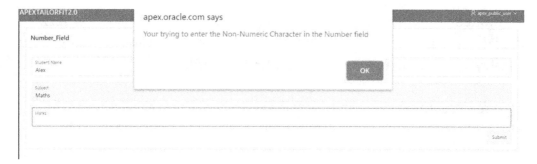

5.2.5 Password

Introduction to Password

The Password field item will render as an HTML Password Form Element.

This item does not display the text entered in a password field but shows up as dots on the screen. This Field helps to prevent others from reading the password on the screen. When creating password items, Oracle recommends using password attributes that do not save session state to prevent the password from being saved in the database in the session state tables.

Configurable Password Item Attributes

Value Required	If select Yes and the page item is visible, Oracle APEX automatically performs a NOT NULL validation when the page is submitted.
Submit when Enter Pressed	If Selected as "Yes" to submit the page when ENTER is pressed, this saves the password in a database table when the page is

	submitted.
	Select "No" to not save the password in a database table.
	The User has to select "Yes" only when the password is needed in session state for use by other pages during the session.
Does not save state	If Select "Yes" to suppress text entered in the field and not save the value in session state.
	For security reasons user should always set this attribute to Yes.

Learning Objective

The Password item renders the content entered in the *"Custom attributes"*as HTML so we can display the Password strength meter, we can build a custom solution using this functionality of Password. Below is a use case for Password:

Use case for Password:

5.2.5.1   Requirement:

Password Strength Meter

Solution: You could achieve this using HTML and JavaScript in Oracle APEX Page *"Function and Global Variable Declaration"* section. Let us see the step by step process to achieve this.

Step 1: Create a page item and set the type as Password.

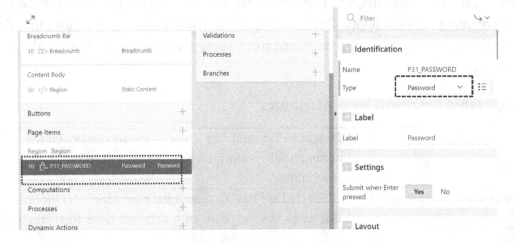

Default Password:

Password Field

Password

To achieve the styles, type in the below CSS in page Inline Section.

```
Inline                                                    ⊅

#passwordStrength {
        height: 10px;
        display: block;
        float: left;
}

.strength0 {
        width: 190px;
        background: #cccccc;
}

.strength1 {
        width: 45px;
        background: #ff0000;
}

.strength2 {
        width: 90px;
```

#Sample Code

```
#passwordStrength {
    height: 10px;
    display: block;
    float: left;
}

.strength0 {
    width: 190px;
    background: #cccccc;
}

.strength1 {
    width: 45px;
    background: #ff0000;
}
```

```
.strength2 {
    width: 90px;
    background: #ff5f5f;
}

.strength3 {
    width: 135px;
    background: #56e500;
}

.strength4 {
    background: #4dcd00;
    width: 160px;
}

.strength5 {
    background: #399800;
    width: 190px;
}
```

Step 2: Add the below script in Page "*Function and Global Variable Declaration*" of the page.

```
Function and Global Variable Declaration                    ↗

function passwordStrengthmeter() {
        var pwd=document.getElementById('P31_PASSWORD');
        var password=document.getElementById("P31_PASSWORD").value;
        var desc=new Array();
        desc[0]="Very Weak";
        desc[1]="Weak";
        desc[2]="Better";
        desc[3]="Medium";
        desc[4]="Strong";
        desc[5]="Strongest";
        var score=0;
        if (password.length > 6) score++;
        if ( ( password.match(/[a-z]/)) && ( password.match(/[A-
Z]/))) score++;
```

#Sample Code

```
function passwordStrengthmeter() {
    var pwd=document.getElementById('P31_PASSWORD');
    var password=document.getElementById("P31_PASSWORD").value;
    var desc=new Array();
    desc[0]="Very Weak";
    desc[1]="Weak";
    desc[2]="Better";
    desc[3]="Medium";
    desc[4]="Strong";
    desc[5]="Strongest";
    var score=0;
    if (password.length> 6) score++;
    if ( (password.match(/[a-z]/)) && ( password.match(/[A-Z]/))) score++;
    if (password.match(/\d+/)) score++;
    if ( password.match(/.[!, @, #, $, %, ^, &, *, ?, _, ~, -, (, )]/)) score++;
    if (password.length> 12) score++;
    document.getElementById("passwordDescription").innerHTML=desc[score];
    if (password.length==0) {
            document.getElementById("passwordDescription").innerHTML='Password    not
entered';
    }
    document.getElementById("passwordStrength").className="strength"+score;
}
```

Step3: Go to the Element advanced custom Attributes of **P31_PASSWORD** Item and paste the following code.

#Sample Code

```
onkeyup="return passwordStrengthmeter();"
```

Step4: Go to the Post Element Text of **P31_PASSWORD** Item and paste the following code.

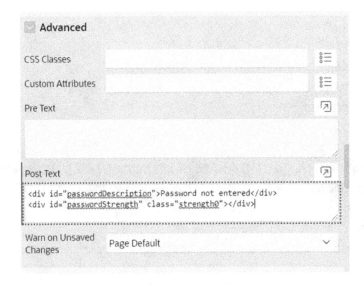

#Sample Code

```
<div id="passwordDescription">Password not entered</div>
<div id="passwordStrength" class="strength0"></div>
```

Output:

Now UI of the Password is as follows:

Password Not Entered:

Password Field

Weak Password:

Password Field

Better Password

Password Field

Medium Password

Password Field

Strong Password

Password Field

5.2.6 Radio Group

Introduction to Radio Group

As the name denotes, the Radio group is a list of radio buttons that provides users list of choices to choose one value at a time. Radio group is similar to list option, in case of having minimumnumber of values then we can go for radio group. If there is huge number of values, then we can go for select list.

Learning Objective

In Radio Group, the value can be set by using LOV or Static values. In the LOV we can specify the display values and value of the page item will be set to when the radio button is selected. We can specify the radio buttons with number of columns to display. Upon the default functionality we can also customize the radio buttons. Below is the use case for radio group and its customization.

Use case for Radio Group:

5.2.6.1 Requirement:

Whilecapturing the student details, we are also capturing the Gender information using the Radio Group. Instead of specifying the Radio Buttons in default manner we need to apply background color and borders for the selected item, on mouse over of the radio group, the items are highlighted with background color.

Solution

Below are the steps to create a simple radio group with the static values and apply the CSS to change the background color and borders.

Step 1: Create a new static region as "Student Details".

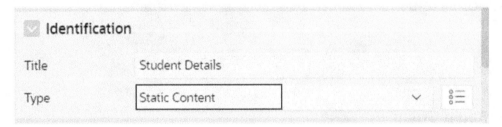

Step 2: Create text field for Student Name, Roll Number and Student Age. For DOB create as Date Picker.

Step 3: Create a new item type as "Radio Group" and set the Label as "Gender. In list of Values, select the type as "Static Values" and Assign the values for the Radio Group.

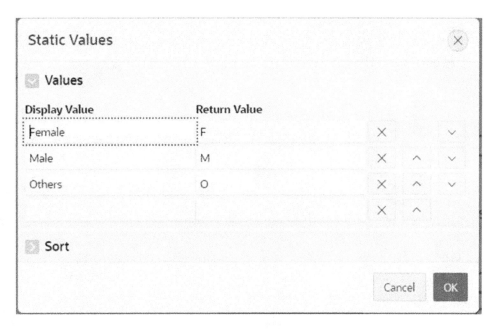

Step 4: On the "Inline" of the Page, type in the below CSS code.

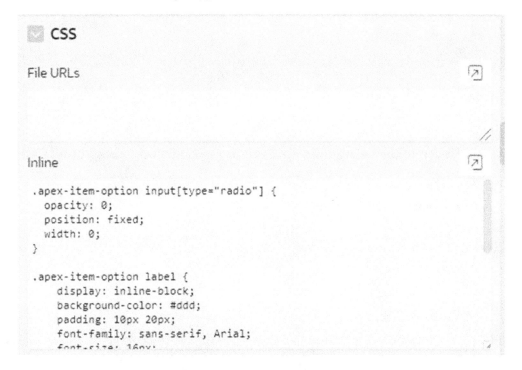

//To add the background color and set the border for the selected item

#Sample Code

```
.apex-item-option input[type="radio"] {
  opacity: 0;
  position: fixed;
  width: 0;
}
.apex-item-option label {
    display: inline-block;
    background-color: #ddd;
    padding: 10px 20px;
    font-family: sans-serif, Arial;
    font-size: 16px;
    border: 2px solid #444;
    border-radius: 4px;
}
.apex-item-option input[type="radio"]:checked + label {
    background-color:#bfb;
    border-color: #4c4;
}
.apex-item-option input[type="radio"]:focus + label {
    border: 2px dashed #444;
}
```

// On Mouse Hover, of the radio group the items are specified with background Color

```
.apex-item-option label:hover {
  background-color: #dfd;
}
```

Click Save and Run the Page.

Output:

Selecting the Value as "Female".

On Mouse over of the value "Others", the "others" value highlighted.

5.2.7 Rich Text Editor

Introduction to Rich Text Editor

The Rich Text Editor item in the Oracle APEX allows editing of formatted text-unlike a simple text area that will enable you to work with plain ASCII text. A rich text editor generates the formatted text as an HTML code and sends it to the APEX page. Many applications store the HTML text directly in a database table.

Learning Objective

The rich text editor extends the ability of a high edit box. It provides for robust formatting of text content, including necessary structural treatments such as lists, format such as drag-and-drop inclusion, bold and italic text and image size.

Use case for Rich Text Editor:

5.2.7.1 Requirement

The Universal theme of Oracle APEX 5.1 provides responsive user interface themes that enables all the item type to be responsive except an item Rich Text Editor. However, this has been fixed from the next version of Oracle APEX 5.1. Let's look how to create a responsive Rich Text Editor in Oracle APEX 5.1.

Solution:

We can achieve this by adding small piece of JavaScript code in the target page of the Oracle APEX. Let us see the step by step process to achieve this.

Step 1: Create an item type Rich Text Editor.

Step 2: Navigate to Advanced section of an item and type in the code given below in the JavaScript Initialization area.

```
JavaScript Initialization Code

function ( configObject ) {
    configObject.uiColor        = "#AADC6E";
    configObject.resize_enabled = false;
/*For other attributes check below link*/

/*https://ckeditor.com/docs/ckeditor4/latest/api/CKEDIT
OR_config.html*/
    return configObject;
}
```

#Sample Code

```
 function (o) {
o.width = $("#P1_TEXT_EDITOR").closest(".t-Form-inputContainer").width() - 5;
o.height = 300;  // Specify your desired item height, in pixels
   return o;
}
```

Step 3: Create a Dynamic action as follows:

Event: Resize

Action: Execute Javascript code

#Sample Code

```
//replace P1_TEXT_EDITOR with your page item
CKEDITOR.instances.P1_TEXT_EDITOR.resize( $("#P1_TEXT_EDITOR").closest(".t-
Form-inputContainer").width() - 5, 300);
```

Step 4: Save and Run the page.

Output:

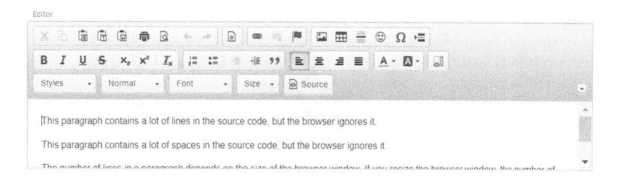

Source: https://joelkallman.blogspot.com/2017/12/how-do-i-create-responsive-rich-text.html

5.2.8 Select List

Introduction to Select List

The Select List field item will render as a HTML Form Element.It defines as that list of values are defined at the item level.

Learning Objective

The Select List Field item can able to render the content entered in the "*Custom attributes*"as HTML so we can set the background color, size and font styles.We can build a customized solution using this functionality of Select List field. Below is a use case for Select List field:

Use case for Select List Field:

For instance, let us consider achieving following functionalities in Select Listfield
- Background Color Change on values.
- Set Styles of Select List.

5.2.8.1 Requirement 1

Background Color Change on values.

Solution:

We can achieve this using HTML and JavaScript in Oracle APEX page "*JavaScript*" section. Let us see the step by step process to achieve this.

Step 1: Create a page item and set the type as Select List Field.

Default Select List Field:

Ticket Status   --Select-- ⌄

Step 2: Add the below script in Page JavaScript" *Execute Page Load*" of the page.

#Sample Code

```
$('#P42_SELECTLIST1').change(function() {
  $(this)
.removeClass('opt-50 opt-51 opt-52')
.addClass('opt-' + $(this).find('option:selected').val());
}).change();
```

To achieve the styles, Paste the below code in Page Inline Section:

#Sample Code

```
#P42_SELECTLIST1.opt-50,
#P42_SELECTLIST1 option[value="50"] {
  background-color: #99CC00;
}
#P42_SELECTLIST1.opt-51,
#P42_SELECTLIST1 option[value="51"] {
  background-color: #FFCC00;
}
#P42_SELECTLIST1.opt-52,
#P42_SELECTLIST1 option[value="52"] {
  background-color: #CC0000;
}
```

Output:

Now UI of the Select List is as follows:

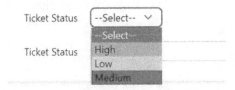

5.2.8.2 Requirement 2:

Set Styles of Select List.

Solution:

We can achieve this using HTML and JavaScript in Oracle APEX page item "*Custom attributes Section*" section. Let us see the step by step process to achieve this.

Step 1: Create a page item and set the type as Select List Field.

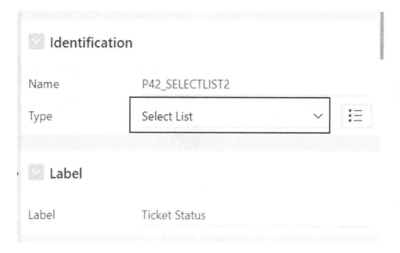

Default Select List Field:

Step 2: Add the below script in Page item advanced "*Custom attributes Section*of the text field.

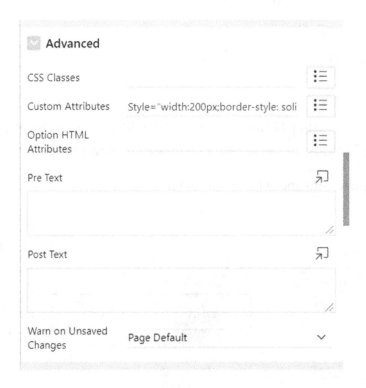

#Sample Code

Style="width:200px;border-style: solid; border-color: red;"

To add More Styles, paste the below code in Inline Section.

#Sample Code

```
.apex-item-select[size="1"] {
    min-height: 2.4rem;
max-height: 2.4rem;
    font-size: medium;
    font-style: italic;
    color: blue;
}
```

Output:

Now UI of the Select List is as follows:

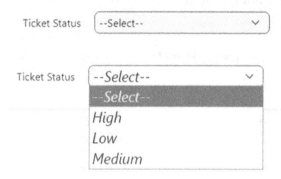

5.2.9 Shuttle

Introduction to Shuttle

APEX Shuttle item is constructed from two primary columns, source and destination. It allows the user to select one or more values. The values shown on the left are the possible values from the source that is available for user selection. The selected values will be shown on the right side of the item. You can choose a value by double-clicking on the possible values on the left side.

Learning Objective

A Shuttle item provides a toolbar placed in the middle that includes features such as Reset, Moves All, Move, remove and Remove All. When submitted, the selected values will be returned to a single colon-delimited string. It can be handled in the two ways:

- Using the INSTR function.
- Using the APEX_UTIL.STRING_TO_TABLE function.

Use case for Shuttle:

5.2.9.1 Requirement:

The Shuttle is helpful when there is a multi-selection required. But it becomes complex in selecting when it has maximum number of values as the possible value from the source. Let us see how to add a filter to Shuttle Item.

Solution:

You could achieve this by adding minimal JavaScript in Oracle APEX. Let us see the step by step process to achieve this.

Step 1: Create a region in the name **Shuttle with filter** and select region type as Static Content.

Step 2: Then, create a Shuttle Item and name it as Shuttle,

Step 3: Navigate to Layout section and map the Region it belongs.

Step 4: Navigate to List of values section and place the select query as given below.

#Sample Code

```
select ename d, empno r from emp
```

Step 5: Now on the same page, navigate to *"Function and Global Variable Declaration"* under JavaScript in the page propertiesand add the code given below:

#Sample Code

```
(function($){
    $.fn.htmldbShuttlefilter=function(options){
      options=$.extend({},{"label":"Filter"},options);
      return this.each(function(i){
       var $self      = $(this)
     ,filterId     = $self.attr("id") + "_FILTER"
     ,$select      = $self.find("select")
     ,shuttleValues = $select.children("option").map(function(){
        return {text:$(this).text(),value:$(this).val(),option:this}
        })
     ,$filter                                                               =
$("<input/>",{"type":"text","value":"","size":"255","autocomplete":"off","id":filterId})
     .keyup(function(){
        var filterval   = new RegExp("^"+$(this).val()+".*","i")
     ,selectedValues = $select.eq(1).children("option").map(function(){
        return $(this).val();
        });
        $select.eq(0).empty();
     $.each(shuttleValues,function(idx,obj){
        if(obj["text"].match(filterval) && $.inArray(obj["value"],selectedValues)<0){
         $select.eq(0).append(obj["option"]);
        }
        });
        })
     .width($self.width());
        $("<div/>",{"css":{"padding-bottom":"5px"}})
     .insertBefore($self)
     .append(
        $("<label/>",{"for":filterId})
     .append($("<span/>",{"css":{"font-weight":"bold"}}).text(options.label))
        )
     .append("<br/>").append($filter);
        $self.find("img[alt='Reset']").click(function(){$filter.val("")});
        });
```

```
    }
})(jQuery);
```

Step 6: Then add the code given below in the "Execute and Page loads" section available in the page property.

#Sample Code

```
//replace P29_SHUTTLE with your page item
$("#P29_SHUTTLE").htmldbShuttlefilter({});
$(".t-Form-itemWrapper").css("display","inline");
```

Step 7: Finally, Save and Run the page.

Output:

The page will look like the below screen shot.

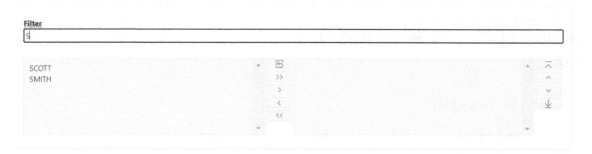

Source:
https://jaris.tilaa.cloud/apex/f?p=BLOG:READ:::NO::ARTICLE:201410131041380630

5.2.10 Text Field

Introduction to Text Field

The Text field item will render as a HTML Form Element.

The text field display the values entered by the user as it is in the screen and the following settings can be applied to the text field.

Text Field Setting

Value Required	If selected as "Yes" and the page item will be visible, Oracle APEX automatically performs a NOT NULL validation when the page is submitted.
Submit when Enter Pressed	If this option is activated by selecting the parameter value as "Yes", then the page item is being submitted when enter is pressed.
Does not save state	If selected as "Yes" then suppresses the text entered the field and does not save the value in session state. For security reasons this parameter should be always made as "Yes".

Learning Objective

The Text Field item can able to render the content entered in the "*Custom attributes*"as HTML so we can display the Upper Case, Lower Case & Caps Lock Indicator. We can build a customized solution using this functionality of Text field. Below is a use case for Text field:

Use case for Text Field:

For instance, let us consider achieving following functionalities in Text field

- Auto Upper-Case Conversion.
- Auto Lower-Case Conversion.
- Caps Lock Indicator.

5.2.10.1 Requirement 1

Auto Upper-Case Conversion.

Solution:

We can achieve this using HTML and JavaScript in Oracle APEX page item "*Custom attributes Section*" section. Let us see the step by step process to achieve this.

Step 1: Create a page item and set the type as *Text Field*.

Identification

Name	P41_TEXTFIELD1
Type	Text Field

Label

Label	Text Field

Default Text Field:

Text Field

Step 2: Add the below script in Page item advanced "*Custom attributes Section*"of the text field.

Advanced

CSS Classes	
Custom Attributes	onkeyup="this.value = this.value.toU
Pre Text	
Post Text	
Warn on Unsaved Changes	Page Default

#Sample Code

```
onkeyup="this.value = this.value.toUpperCase();"
```

Output:

Now UI of the Text Field is as follows:

Text Field	DOYENSYS

Change Text to Auto Uppercase

5.2.10.2 Requirement 2

Auto Lower-Case Conversion.

Solution:

You could achieve this using HTML and JavaScript in Oracle APEX page item "*Custom attributes Section*" section. Let us see the step by step process to achieve this.

Step 1: Create a page item and set the type as *Text Field*.

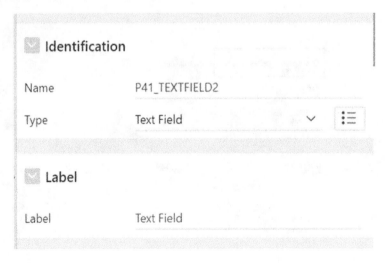

Default Text Field:

Text Field

Step 2: Add the below script in Page item advanced *"Custom attributes Section"*of the text field.

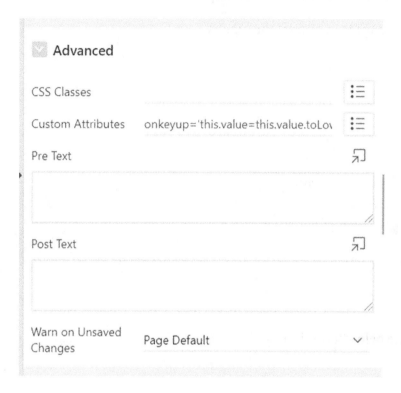

#Sample Code

```
onkeyup='this.value=this.value.toLowerCase();'
```

Output:

Now UI of the Text Field is as follows:

Text Field [doyensys]

Change Text to Auto Lowercase

5.2.10.3 Requirement 3

Caps Lock Indicator.

Solution:

You could achieve this using HTML and JavaScript in Oracle APEX page item "*Custom attributes Section*" section. Let us see the step by step process to achieve this.

Step 1: Create a page item and set the type as *Text Field*.

Identification	
Name	P41_TEXTFIELD3
Type	Text Field

Label	
Label	Text Field

Default Text Field:

Text Field

Step 2: Add the below script in Page JavaScript "*Function and Global Variable Declaration*" of the Page.

JavaScript

File URLs

Function and Global Variable Declaration

```
function capLock(e){
 kc = e.keyCode?e.keyCode:e.which;
 sk = e.shiftKey?e.shiftKey:((kc == 16)?true:false);
 if(((kc >= 65 && kc <= 90) && !sk)||((kc >= 97 && kc
<= 122) && sk))
   document.getElementById('divMayus').style.visibility
```

Execute when Page Loads

#Sample Code

```
function capLock(e){
 kc = e.keyCode?e.keyCode:e.which;
sk = e.shiftKey?e.shiftKey:((kc == 16)?true:false);
if(((kc >= 65 && kc <= 90) && !sk)||((kc >= 97 && kc <= 122) &&sk))
document.getElementById('divMayus').style.visibility = 'visible';
 else
document.getElementById('divMayus').style.visibility = 'hidden';
 }
```

Step 3: Add the below script in Page item advanced "*Custom attributes Section*" of the text field and also add the below script in "*Post text*" Section.

#Sample Code

```
onkeypress="capLock(event)"
```

Post Text:

#Sample Code

```
<div id="divMayus" style="visibility:hidden;color:red;">Caps Lock is on.</div>
```

Output:

Now UI of the Text Field is as follows:

Text Field [doyensys]

Check CapsLock On

Text Field [DOYENSYS] Caps Lock is on.

Check CapsLock On

5.2.11 Text Field with Autocomplete

Introduction to Text Field with Auto Complete

Text field with auto completedisplays a list of valuesbased on the LOV and user can enter the required text, for processing that are not on the list. Whenever user type a character it will list all the possible words from LOV.

Learning Objective

Text field with auto complete is like a select list. But in select list we can't type and search. In text with auto complete we can search the values by entering the text and if the list is long then text with auto complete will be very helpful. We can also customize the text with auto complete and below is the use case for it.

Use case for Text Field with Auto Complete:

5.2.11.1 Requirement

By default, in Text with auto complete, we can select a single value from the List and let us consider we have a requirement to select multiple values from the list in text with auto complete option.

Solution

To select the multiple employee names from the list with text field auto complete option, use JavaScript. Let us see a step by step process for the below use cases.

*Step 1:*Create a new item "**P22_Employee**" and assign the item as text field with auto complete.

*Step 2:*Create a new Application Process with the below details.

Process Point: Ajax Callback: Run this application process when requested by a page process.

Name: EMP_DTLS

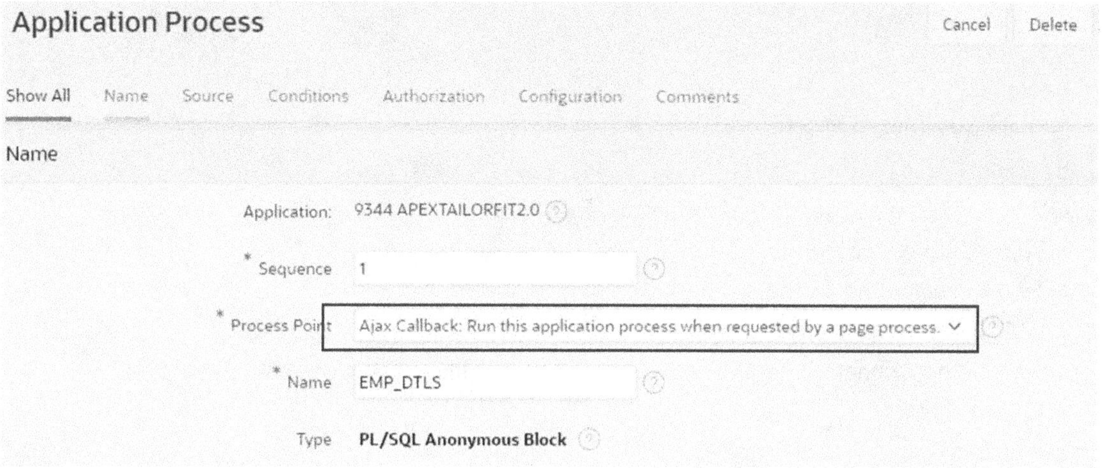

Step 3: Place the below PL/SQL code in a Source field.

```
* PL/SQL Code ?

 1  declare
 2  lv_rslt varchar2(32000);
 3  begin
 4  OWA_UTIL.mime_header ('text/xml', FALSE);
 5     HTP.p ('Cache-Control: no-cache');
 6     HTP.p ('Pragma: no-cache');
 7     OWA_UTIL.http_header_close;
 8  select listagg(Ename,',')within group(order by empno) into lv_rslt from emp;
 9  HTP.prn(lv_rslt);
10  exception
11  when others then
12  HTP.prn(sqlerrm);
13  end;
```

#*Sample Code*

```
declare
lv_rslt varchar2(32000);
begin
OWA_UTIL.mime_header ('text/xml', FALSE);
HTP.p ('Cache-Control: no-cache');
HTP.p ('Pragma: no-cache');
OWA_UTIL.http_header_close;
select listagg(Ename,',')within group(order by empno) into lv_rslt from emp;
HTP.prn(lv_rslt);
exception
when others then
HTP.prn(sqlerrm);
end;
```

Step 4: Place the URL's in JavaScript File URL's of the Page.

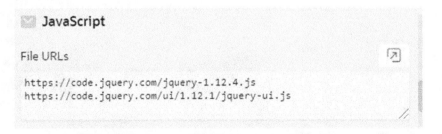

#Sample Code

```
https://code.jquery.com/jquery-1.12.4.js
https://code.jquery.com/ui/1.12.1/jquery-ui.js
```

Step 5: The below is the Customized code to select multiple values from the list with auto complete option. Place the code in "*Function and Global Variable Declaration*" of the Page. Then click Save and Run the Page.

```
Function and Global Variable Declaration                    ⌐⊅⌐

$(function() {
    apex.server.process(
        "EMP_DTLS", {}, {
            dataType: 'text',
            success: function(pData) {

                var availableTags = pData.split(',');
                console.log(availableTags);

                function split(val) {
                    return val.split(/,\s*/);
```

#Sample Code

```
$(function() {
apex.server.process(
     "EMP_DTLS", {}, {
dataType: 'text',
        success: function(pData) {
            var availableTags = pData.split(',');
            console.log(availableTags);
            function split(val) {
                return val.split(/,\s*/);
            }
            function extractLast(term) {
                return split(term).pop();
            }
            $("#P22_EMPLOYEE")
```

// don't navigate away from the field on tab when selecting an item

```
.on("keydown", function(event) {
        if (event.keyCode === $.ui.keyCode.TAB&&
            $(this).autocomplete("instance").menu.active) {
event.preventDefault();
        }
    })
.autocomplete({
minLength: 0,
        source: function(request, response) {
```

// delegate back to autocomplete, but extract the last term

```
response($.ui.autocomplete.filter(
availableTags, extractLast(request.term)));
        },
        focus: function() {
```

// prevent value inserted on focus

```
            return false;
        },
        select: function(event, ui) {
            var terms = split(this.value);
```

// remove the current input

```
terms.pop();
```

// add the selected item

```
terms.push(ui.item.value);
```

// add placeholder to get the comma-and-space at the end

```
terms.push("");
this.value = terms.join(", ");
            return false;
        }
    });
    }
    }
```

```
  );
});
```

Output

Here the Input Text is "C", it will display the list of employee name with Character "C" and select the employee name as "SCOTT".

Enter another search character as "A" and it will display the list of employee name with Character "A" and Select Employee name is "ALLEN". In this similar we can select multiple items from the list.

5.2.12 Text Area

Introduction to Text Area

A text area can hold a multi-line text input. The text area is often used in a form to collect user inputs such as comments or reviews. The text area can carry an infinite number of characters and the text can be rendered in a fixed-width. The size of a text area is defined by the attribute's cols and rows.

Learning Objective

The height and width of Text Area can be controlled by editing the Height, Width and Maximum width attributes in Oracle APEX. Creating Text area in Oracle APEX can be done using two ways by Creating Item/using Text area function.

Use case for Text Area:

5.2.12.1 Requirement:

There is an inbuilt option called auto height in the Text Area properties which specify whether the height of the text area varies based on the amount of text displayed. Here, height will be auto adjusted only during the display i.e. It won't help to auto increase/decrease height during run time. Let us see how to auto increase/decrease height during run time.

Solution:

You could achieve this by adding minimal JavaScript in Oracle APEX. Let us see the step by step process to achieve this.

Step 1:Create a region in the name **Text Area** and select region type as Static Content.

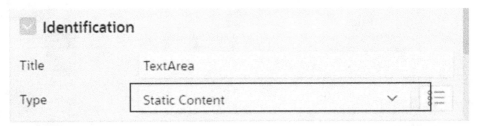

Step 2: Then, create a Text Area and name it as Text Area.

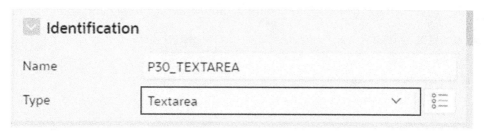

Step 3: Now on the same page, navigate to *"Function and Global Variable Declaration"* under JavaScript in the page properties and add the code given below.

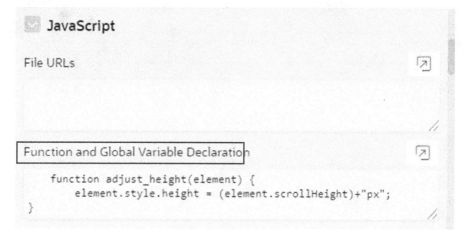

#Sample Code

```
function adjust_height(element) {
element.style.height = (element.scrollHeight)+"px";
}
```

Step 4: Then add the code given below in the "Execute and Page loads" section available in the page property.

#Sample Code

```
//replace P30_TEXTAREA with your page item
$("#P30_TEXTAREA").attr("oninput","adjust_height(this)");
```

Step 5: Finally, Save and Run the page.

Output:

The page will look like the below screen shot.

TextArea

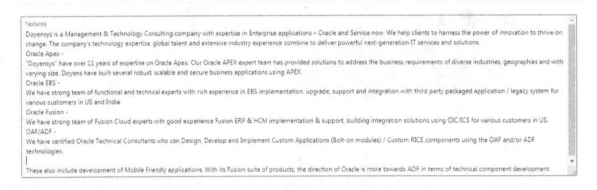

5.3 BUTTONS

Introduction to Button

Button in Oracle APEX can perform four types of actions like submitting a page, redirect to another page in the same application, add custom URL and define a dynamic response.

Creating Button in Oracle APEX can be done either using Component view or Tree View in Universal theme.

Learning Objective

When we are designing our application, we can use the buttons to direct users to a specific page or URL or to post or process information. We can add CSS to button to enhance the look and feel of button on form/report screen.

Use case for Button:

5.3.1   Requirement 1:

Usually, the link column in the Classic/IR report will appear similar to the other columns in the report, until user move's the cursor over the link column. So, let us have the requirement to have button type appearance for link column in the report.

Solution:

We can achieve this by adding minimal CSS in the link column of Classic/IR report. Let us see the step by step process to achieve this.

Step 1: Create a region in the name **Employee Report** and select region type as Classic Report.

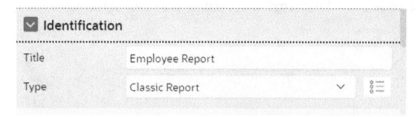

Step 2: Select source type as SQL Query and place your code.

Code Editor - SQL Query

```
1 SELECT dname department, ename Name , job , sal Salary
2     FROM emp e, dept d
3     WHERE e.deptno = d.deptno
4 order by 1, 2
```

#Sample Code

SELECT dname department, enameName , job , sal Salary

```
FROM emp e, dept d
WHERE e.deptno = d.deptno
order by 1, 2
```

Step 3: Click on the column for which you want to set a link. (Here, for an example, let me choose column **Name** to have a link and change column type from plain text to link as in the below screen shot)

Step 4: Then, navigate to the link section for the same column and set up a link and type in the below CSS code in the Link Attributes section as shown in the screen shot.

#Sample Code

```
class="t-Button t-Button--hot"
```

Step 5: Save and Run the page.

Output: Below screen shot shows the difference in the style of the Regular Check box and Customized Check box.

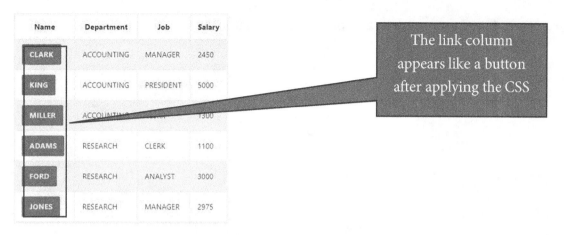

The link column appears like a button after applying the CSS

Source : https://apex.oracle.com/pls/apex/f?p=42:6100:::NO:::

5.3.1.1 Requirement 2:

Adding effects to the items in the screen will always attracts the user to your website or application. Let us have the same as a requirement for the Button in the Oracle APEX.

Solution:

We can achieve this by adding minimal CSS in Oracle APEX. Let us see the step by step process to achieve this.

Step 1:Create a region with the name **"Button"** and select region type as "Static Content".

Identification

Title	BUTTON
Type	Static Content

Step 2: Create a Button as shown below.

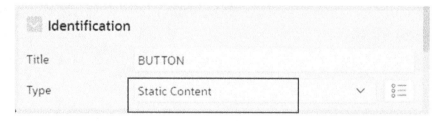

Identification

Button Name	SAMPLE_BUTTON
Label	Sample Button

Step 3: Navigate to Layout section and map the Region it belongs.

Step 4: Go to Appearance section of the Button and enable as HOT.

Step 5: Go to Advance section and assign a static id as **GLOW_BTN.**

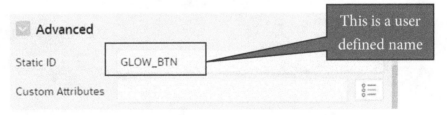

Step 6: Now on the same page, navigate to "Inline" under CSS section in the page propertiesand include the code given below.

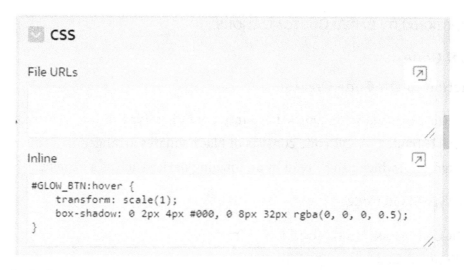

#Sample Code

```
#GLOW_BTN:hover {
    transform: scale(1);
    box-shadow: 0 2px 4px #000, 0 8px 32px rgba(0, 0, 0, 0.5);
}
```

Step 7: Save and Run the page.

Output:

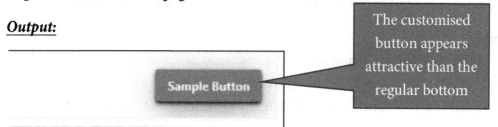

The customised button appears attractive than the regular bottom

5.4 Functionality based Customizations

5.4.1 QR Code

Introduction to QR Code Creator

A QR code (abbreviated from Quick Response code) is a type of matrix barcode (or two-dimensional barcode). A QR code consists of black squares arranged in a square grid on a white background, which can be read by an imaging device such as a camera.

Different Type of QR Code

- QR Code Model1 and Model2
- Micro QR Code
- Frame QR Code
- SQRC Code
- iQR Code

We can create any type of QR code based on various business requirement. For our experiment we have taken QR Code Model1 and Model2.

Few use cases to bring the QR code in your business application are listed below.

- **Reports**
  Most of the business are being effectively managed and operated with the help of various reports. We can include the QR code in such reports and provide additional information to the intended user by hiding the same information from others.

- **Login**
  Now a days in most of the business premises, the gate entry and exit has been controlled using bio metric data, however, our business application are still following the traditional way of login using the username and password. Using the QR code we can make the login to our business application more secured. We can send a onetime QR code for each login similar to OTP (One Time Password), using which the user can login in to the application. In this way even the user will not know what their password is and hence they will not be able to share it to others.

- **File Transfer**

  QR code also facilitates to convert your file in QR code format and simply by scanning the QR code the file can be transferred from one device to another.

- **Minimizes Data Entry**

  If a specific data needs to be reused my many peoples in many occasions, instead of share the raw data, we can convert the same into QR Code and share it the intended users, using which they will be able to input the required information to your business application just by scanning the QR code instead of manually entering the information again and again.

- **Executing Database Objects**

  Using QR code we can read the scripts and execute the same in the Oracle database. This can be effectively implemented in scenarios where you want to allow the users execute required scripts directly in the database without sharing the database credentials.

Learning Objective

The objective of this section is to provide our insight of creating a QR code in Oracle APEX application.

The static content renders the content entered in the "*Source*"attribute as HTML so we can display the same in the application. Since it is like a white canvas, we can build a customized solution using this functionality of static content. Below is a use case for Static Content:

Use Case

5.4.1.1 Requirement

Converting the user input as QR code and preserving the same in Database for various future use.

Solution:

We can achieve this using HTML and JavaScript in Oracle APEX static region. Let us see the step by step process to achieve this.

Step1: Create two static regions and one Interactive or classic Report.

Region 1:

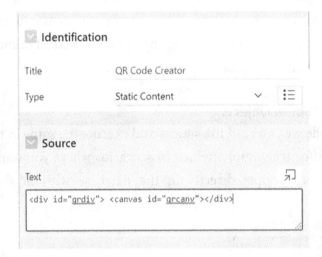

#Sample Code

```
<div id="qrdiv"><canvas id="qrcanv"></div>
```

Region 2: Download Region

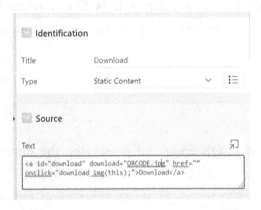

#Sample Code

```
<a id="download" download="QRCODE.jpg" href=""
onclick="download_img(this);">Download</a>
```

Region 3: Interactive Report

#Sample Code

```
select QRCODE_ID,

    QRCODE_VALUE,

    FILENAME,

    MIMETYPE

    (dbms_lob.getlength(FILECONTENT))  download

from DOY_FLEXR_QR_CODETBL

order by 1 desc
```

Note: "DOY_FLEXR_QR_CODETBL" is a custom Table & user can able to use their own Tables.

Step2: We need to create two page items as Text field (Input) and Hidden Item.

Step3: In the page, On the "*Function and Global Variable Declaration*" of the page, type in the below JavaScript function code.

```
JavaScript

File URLs

Function and Global Variable Declaration

// alignment pattern
adelta = [
  0, 11, 15, 19, 23, 27, 31, // force 1 pat
  16, 18, 20, 22, 24, 26, 28, 20, 22, 24, 24, 26, 28,
28, 22, 24, 24,
  26, 26, 28, 28, 24, 24, 26, 26, 26, 28, 28, 24, 26,
26, 26, 28, 28
  ];

// version block
vpat = [
  0xc94, 0x5bc, 0x299, 0x4d3, 0xbf6, 0x762, 0x847
```

Execute when Page Loads

#Sample Code

Please go to the link http://blogs.doyensys.com/qr-code-creator-oracle-apex/ for downloading the entire script.

Step4:We need to create two dynamic actions as follows:

Dynamic Action 1:

- **On Event**: Page Load

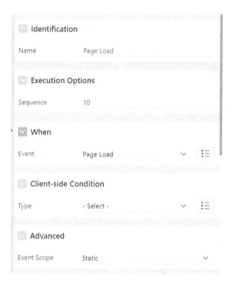

- **Action**: Execute JavaScript Code: setupqr();

Dynamic Action 2:

- **Event:** Change of Input Item

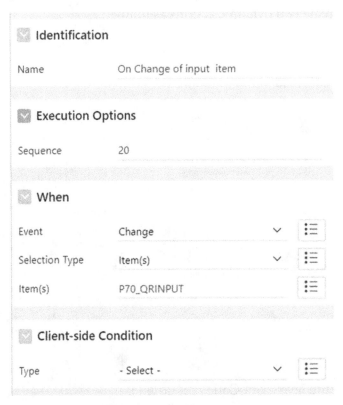

- **Action:** Execute JavaScript code:doqr();

- Execute JavaScript code captureToCanvas();

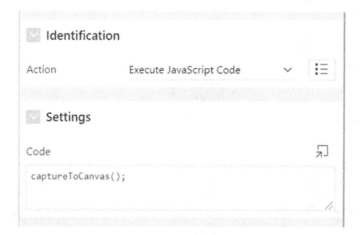

- **Execute Plsql Code:**

#Sample Code

```
DECLARE
lv_qrcode_idNUMBER;
v_resultBLOB;
v_clobCLOB := replace(:p70_image_base64,'data:image/png;base64,','');
BEGIN
v_result := base64decode(v_clob);
   SELECT
nvl(MAX(qrcode_id),0) + 1
   INTO lv_qrcode_id
   FROM
doy_flexr_qr_codetbl;
begin
   INSERT INTO doy_flexr_qr_codetbl (
qrcode_id,
qrcode_value,
     filename,
mimetype,
filecontent,
created_by,
created_date
```

```
    ) VALUES (
lv_qrcode_id,
:p70_qrinput,
    'QRCODE' || lv_qrcode_id||'.jpeg',
    'image/jpeg',
v_result,
    :app_user,
    SYSDATE
  );
end;
END;
```

- **Refresh Classic/IR Report.**

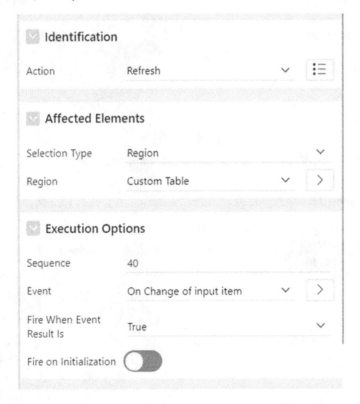

Output:

Now UI of the QR Code as follows:

QR Code Creator

Input Value   Doyensys

5.4.2 Unsaved Page Toggling and Side Navigation on Mouse Over

Navigation serves the purpose of redirecting the users to the relevant page based on the user selection. Top and Sidebar are the two types of navigation. Navigation structure for your application can be defined in the Navigation Menu and it is based on the List component in APEX. Navigation control can be dynamic (based on a SQL query) or static (based on static list entries).

Use case for Navigation:

We shall review 2 scenarios

- Warn on Unsaved Changes (Oracle APEX has an inbuilt feature for this from 18C release onwards).
- Hide and show of Navigation.

Warn on unsaved Changes:

When user navigate away from a form before saving the data, then user can be provided with an alert / warning message.

Hide and show of Navigation:

When we use side navigation, to view full screen / page, the collapse button should be clicked to hide / show the page navigation menu.Instead we shall apply a custom code to automatically hide / show the navigation bar on mouse over.

5.4.2.1   Requirement 1:

Warn on unsaved Changes: We can achieve this using Execute JavaScript functions. Let us see the step by step process to achieve this.

Solution:

Step 1: Create a Global Page as "Zero" and create a Static Content Region.

Place the below sample code into the Static Content Source Section.

```
1  <script type="text/javascript">
2
3  function Navigationalert() {
4  var fields = document.getElementById('wwvFlowForm').elements;
5  for (var i=0; i<fields.length; i++) {
6  $x(fields[i]).onchange = function () {
7  window.unsaved=1;
8  }
9  }
10 }
11 window.unsaved = '';
12 window.onbeforeunload = function() {
13 return window.unsaved ? 'There may be unsaved changes to your data.' : undefined;
14 }
15 </script>
```

#Sample Code

```
<script type="text/javascript">
function Navigationalert() {
var fields = document.getElementById('wwvFlowForm').elements;
for (var i=0; i<fields.length; i++) {
$x(fields[i]).onchange = function () {
window.unsaved=1;
}
}
}
window.unsaved = '';
window.onbeforeunload = function() {
return window.unsaved ? 'There may be unsaved changes to your data.' : undefined;
}
</script>
```

Step2: Create a Dynamic action and set when "Event"condition as "Change".

Identification	
Page:	**0. Global Page - Desktop**
* Name	Change
* Sequence	10

When	
* Event	Change
* Selection Type	jQuery Selector
* jQuery Selector	.a-TreeView-node--leaf
Condition	- No Condition -

Jquery Selector: .a-TreeView-node--leaf

Action: Execute JavaScript Code

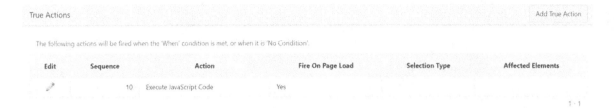

#Sample Code

Execute JavaScript Code: Navigationalert();

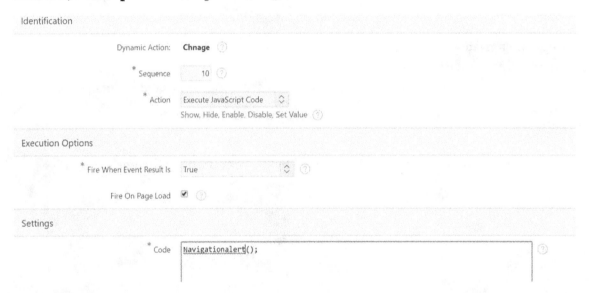

Identification

Dynamic Action:	**Chnage**	
* Sequence	10	
* Action	Execute JavaScript Code	
	Show, Hide, Enable, Disable, Set Value	

Execution Options

* Fire When Event Result Is	True
Fire On Page Load	☑

Settings

* Code	Navigationalert();

Output:

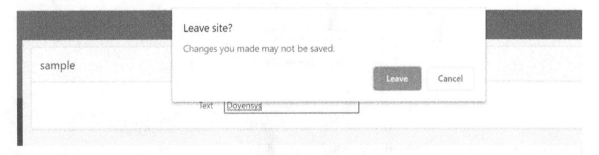

Leave site?

Changes you made may not be saved.

sample

Text | Doyensys

5.4.2.2   Requirement 2:

Hide and show of Navigation: You could achieve this using JavaScript. Let us see the step by step process to achieve this.

Solution:

Step 1: Create a Global Page *page 0*. We create global page since we want the action to be reflected throughout the application.

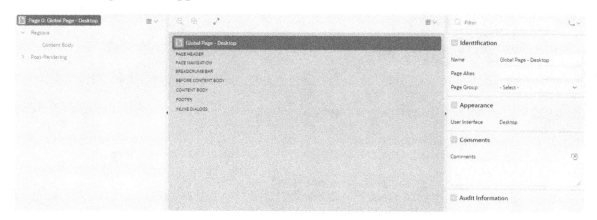

Step2: Create dynamic action On Page Load.

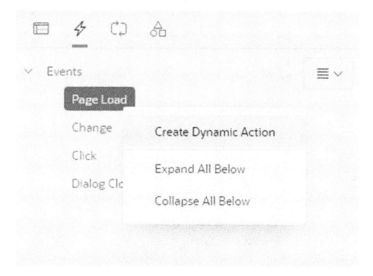

Step 3:Create True Action as Execute JavaScript and Paste the following code.

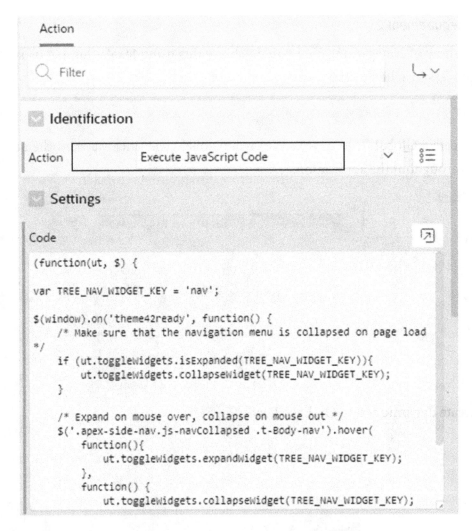

#*Sample Code*

For APEX Version below 19

```
(function(ut, $) {
  var TREE_NAV_WIDGET_KEY = 'nav';
  $(window).on('theme42ready', function() {
    if (ut.toggleWidgets.isExpanded(TREE_NAV_WIDGET_KEY)) {
ut.toggleWidgets.collapseWidget(TREE_NAV_WIDGET_KEY);
    }
/* Expand on mouse over, collapse on mouse out */
```

```
        $('.apex-side-nav.js-navCollapsed .t-Body-nav').hover(
function() {
ut.toggleWidgets.expandWidget(TREE_NAV_WIDGET_KEY);
        },
function() {
ut.toggleWidgets.collapseWidget(TREE_NAV_WIDGET_KEY);
        } );  });
})(apex.theme42, apex.jQuery);
```

For APEX Version higher than 19

```
(function($) {

    $(window).on('theme42ready', function() {

/* Make sure that the navigation menu is collapsed on page load */

        if ($('.t-PageBody').hasClass('js-navExpanded')) {
          $('#t_Button_navControl').click();
        }

/* Expand on mouse over, collapse on mouse out */

        $('.apex-side-nav .t-Body-nav').hover(
function() {
            //only expand if the side menu is collapsed
            $('.t-PageBody:not(.js-navExpanded) #t_Button_navControl').click();
        },
function() {
            $('#t_Button_navControl').click();
        });
    });
})(apex.jQuery);
```

Once done the screen should look like this. And the Collapse mode should be Icon in the Navigation menu of user interface.

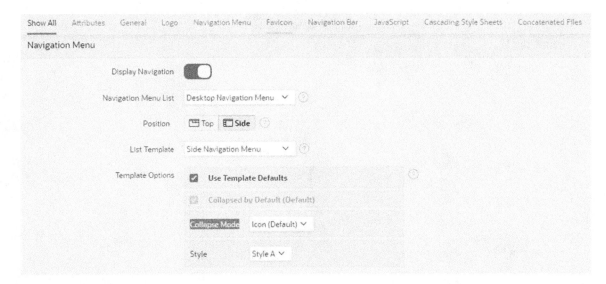

Output:

Now Navigation bar is as follows:

Hidden

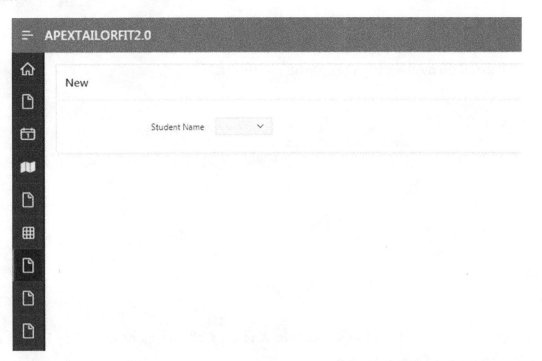

Full view

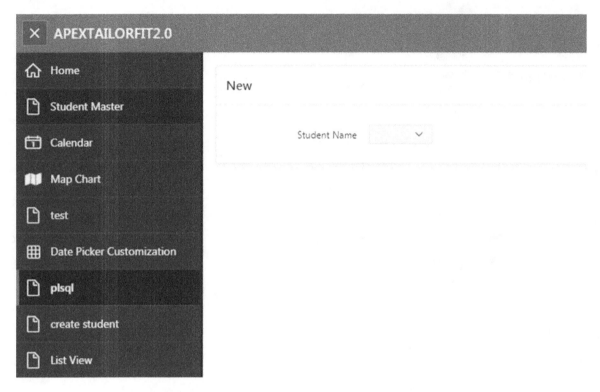

5.4.3 Login Page - Dynamic Background Changer

Introduction to Login Page

When the user creating an application, the login page is automatically created. The Login page is created based on the Oracle APEX login API credentials verification and session registration. We can also able to create Login page based on our business requirements.

Learning Objective

Login Page - Dynamic Background Changer.

Use case for Auto Background changer in login page

5.4.3.1 Requirement:

Login Page with Auto Background Changer, We can achieve this by using simple CSS Classes. Let us see the step by step process to achieve this.

Solution:

Step 1: Create an application and it will automatically create a Login Page.

Import the Images into the Shared Components "*Static Files*" section and refer those images into the CSS Section.

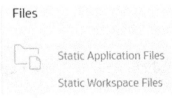

#Sample Code

```
#APP_IMAGES#Image1.jpg
```

Step 2: Place the below sample code into the Page CSS "*Inline*" Section.

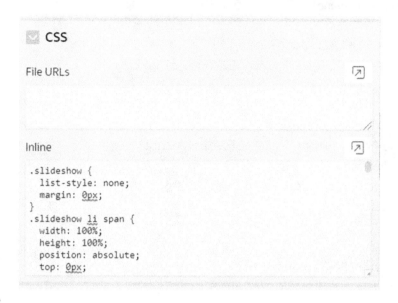

#*Sample Code*

```
.slideshow {
  list-style: none;
  margin: 0px;
}
.slideshow li span {
  width: 100%;
  height: 100%;
  position: absolute;
  top: 0px;
  left: 0px;
color: transparent;
  background-size: cover;
  background-position: 50% 50%;
  background-repeat: none;
  opacity: 0;
  z-index: 0;
  -webkit-backface-visibility: hidden;
backface-visibility: hidden;
  -webkit-animation: imageAnimation 40s linear infinite 0s;
```

```css
  -moz-animation: imageAnimation 40s linear infinite 0s;
  animation: imageAnimation 40s linear infinite 0s;
}
.slideshowli:nth-child(1) span {
  background-image: url(#APP_IMAGES#Image1.jpg);
}

.slideshowli:nth-child(2) span {
  background-image: url(#APP_IMAGES#image2.jpg);
  -webkit-animation-delay: 10s;
  -moz-animation-delay: 10s;
  animation-delay: 10s;
}

.slideshowli:nth-child(3) span {
  background-image: url(#APP_IMAGES#image3.jpg);
  -webkit-animation-delay: 20s;
  -moz-animation-delay: 20s;
  animation-delay: 20s;
}

.slideshowli:nth-child(4) span {
  background-image: url(#APP_IMAGES#image4.jpg);
  -webkit-animation-delay: 30s;
  -moz-animation-delay: 30s;
  animation-delay: 30s;
}

@-webkit-keyframes imageAnimation {
  0% {
    opacity: 0;
    -webkit-animation-timing-function: ease-in;
  }
  12.5% {
    opacity: 1;
    -webkit-animation-timing-function: ease-out;
```

```
  }
  25% {
    opacity: 1;
  }
  37.5% {
    opacity: 0;
  }
  100% {
    opacity: 0;
  }
}
@-moz-keyframes imageAnimation {
  0% {
    opacity: 0;
    -moz-animation-timing-function: ease-in;
  }
  12.5% {
    opacity: 1;
    -moz-animation-timing-function: ease-out;
  }
  25% {
    opacity: 1;
  }
  37.5% {
    opacity: 0;
  }
  100% {
    opacity: 0;
  }
}
@keyframes imageAnimation {
  0% {
    opacity: 0;
    -webkit-animation-timing-function: ease-in;
    -moz-animation-timing-function: ease-in;
    animation-timing-function: ease-in;
```

```
  }
  12.5% {
    opacity: 1;
    -webkit-animation-timing-function: ease-out;
    -moz-animation-timing-function: ease-out;
    animation-timing-function: ease-out;
  }
  25% {
    opacity: 1;
  }
  37.5% {
    opacity: 0;
  }
  100% {
    opacity: 0;
  }
}


.no-cssanimations .slideshow li span {
  opacity: 1;
}
```

Step 3: Copy & Paste the below code into Page "*Header and Footer*" Section.

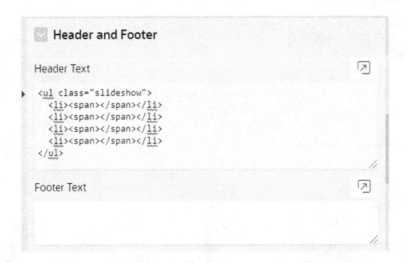

#Sample Code

```
<ul class="slideshow">
<li><span></span></li>
<li><span></span></li>
<li><span></span></li>
<li><span></span></li>
</ul>
```

Output:

Now the UI of Login Page appears with the custom image we have implemented.

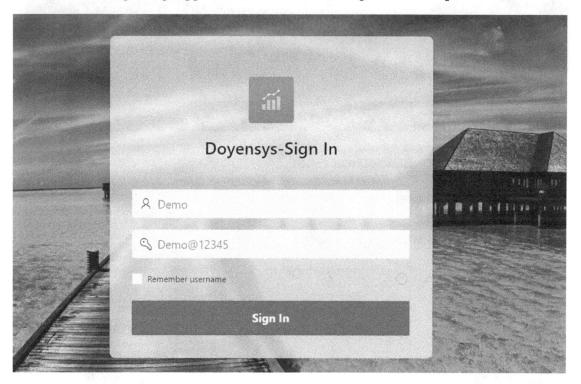

5.4.4 Instant Row Deletion in Reports

Learning Objective

The Classic / Interactive report has the Column link option, so we can display the link as Delete Option and we can build a customized solution using this functionality of Classic/Interactive Report. Below is a use case for Report:

Use case for Instant Row Deletion in Report

5.4.4.1 Requirement:

Instant Row deletion of report.

Solution:

We can achieve this using Column Level Dynamic actions in Oracle APEX Classic report / Interactive report. Let us see the step by step process to achieve this.

Step 1: We must create Classic Report by using a query.

Region1:

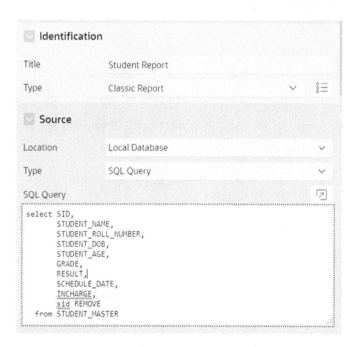

#Sample Code

```
select SID,
     STUDENT_NAME,
     STUDENT_ROLL_NUMBER,
     STUDENT_DOB,
     STUDENT_AGE,
     GRADE,
     RESULT,
     SCHEDULE_DATE,
     INCHARGE,
sid REMOVE
  from STUDENT_MASTER
```

Step 2:Create a page item & set the type as "*Hidden*".

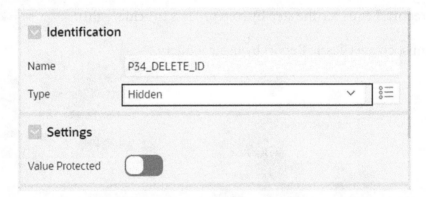

Step 3: In the classic report, Select the column **REMOVE** and set the type as "*Link*".

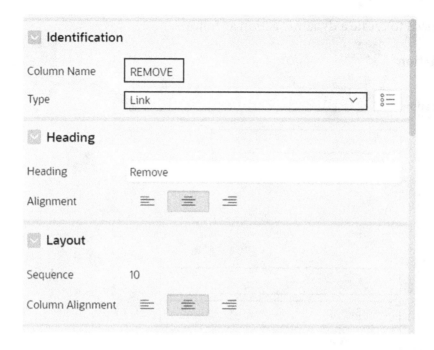

We need to add a link column to your report for the delete icon with the following attributes:

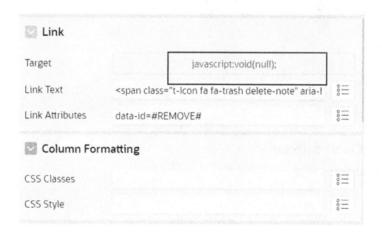

Link Target: URL
URL: javascript:void(null);
Link Text: <span class="t-Icon fa fa-trash delete-note" aria-hidden="true"></span>
Link Attributes: data-id=#REMOVE#

Step 4: We need to create a dynamic action as follows:

Dynamic Action

On Event: Click
Selection Type: jQuery Selector
jQuery Selector: .delete-note

We need to create four true actions as follows:

Action 1:

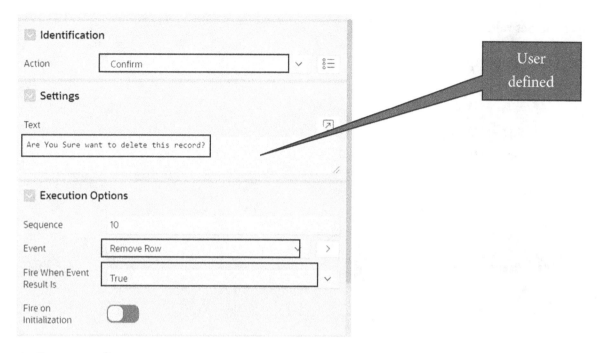

Action: confirm

Action 2:

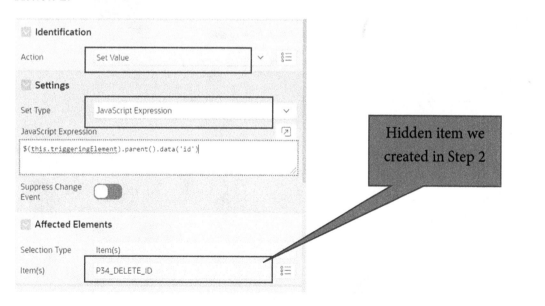

Action: Set value

Set Type: JavaScript expression

#Sample Code

```
$(this.triggeringElement).parent().data('id')
```
Affected Elements: Selection Type

Item Name: P34_DELETE_ID

Action 3:

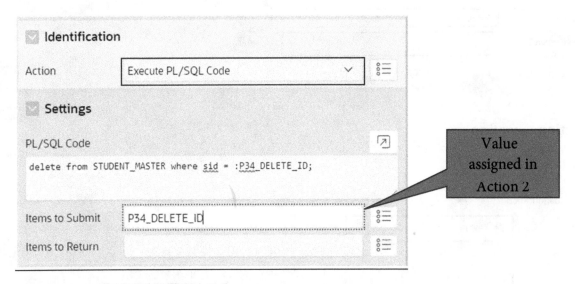

Action: Execute PLSQL Code

#Sample Code

```
delete from STUDENT_MASTER where sid= :P34_DELETE_ID;
```
Items to submit: P34_DELETE_ID

Action 4:

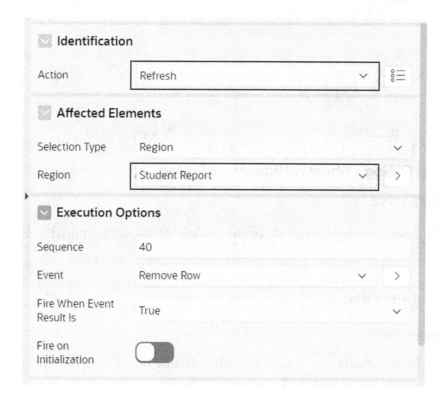

Action: Refresh Classic/Interactive Report

Output:

Now UI of the Instant Row Deletion as follows:

Student Report

Sid ↑↓	Student Name	Student Roll Number	Student Dob	Student Age	Grade	Result	Schedule Date	Incharge	Remove
1	Alex	1	6/2/2005	15	4		6/21/2020		🗑
2	KING	2	6/4/2005	15	1		6/22/2020	1	🗑
3	Martin	3	6/20/2005	15	2		6/24/2020	1	🗑
4	Stephen	4	6/12/2005	15	3		6/23/2020	1	🗑

1 - 4

5.4.5 Modal Dialog - Show & Hide Inline Dialog

Learning Objective

Oracle APEX offers a template called "Inline Dialog" to show the modal Dialog within the page.

Use case for Inline dialog

5.4.5.1 Requirement:

Show & Hide Inline Dialog and closing the Inline Dialog by clicking anywhere in the page.

Solution:

We can achieve this Show & Hide Inline dialog and closing the inline dialog by clicking outside the dialog box using Static ID & simple JavaScript. Let us see the step by step process to achieve this.

Step 1:We must create a region named as "Region" and create a button, assigned to that region.

Region 1:

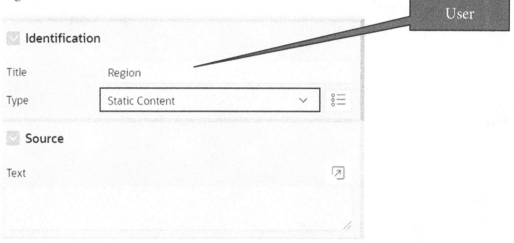

Button:

Step 2:Create another region named as "Dialog" and set the template as "Inline Dialog" in Appearance Section.

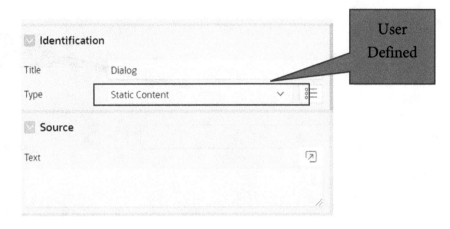

Appearance:

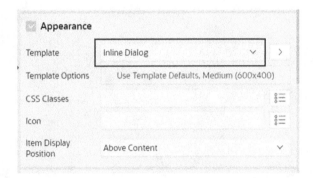

Step 3: Set the Static ID as "REG1" for that region "Dialog" in Advanced Section.

Step 4: Go to the behavior section of button "Open" and set the action as "Redirect to URL" and paste the below java script code in target section.

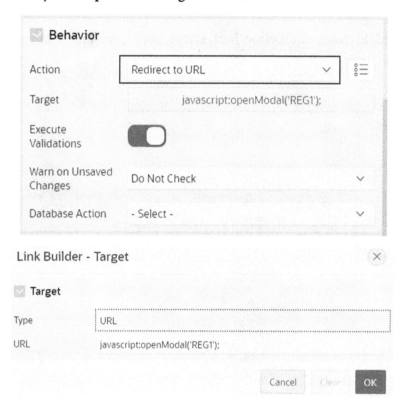

#*Sample Code*

```
javascript:openModal('REG1');
```

To Close the Dialog, we need to use below sample code.

```
javascript:closeModal(REG1);
```

To Pass the parameters values to the Dialog,we need to use below sample code.

```
javascript:$s('P1_REGID',2106);openModal('REG1');
```
OR

```
javascript:$s('P1_REGID',$v('P1_REGID2'));openModal('REG1');
```
OR

```
javascript:$s('P1_REGID','#REGID#');openModal('REG1');
```

Inline Dialog Click Outside:

Step 1: We need to paste the below Java script code into page "*Function and Global Declaration*" section.

#Sample Code

```
function closeDialogClickOutside(elem){
    $('.ui-widget-overlay').click(function(){
      $(elem).dialog('close');
    });
}
```

Step 2: Create a page as "Modal Dialog" and paste the below java script code in Dialog "Attributes" Section.

#Sample Code

```
open: function( event, ui ) { closeDialogClickOutside(this); }
```

Output:

When the user clicks the "Open" Button, it will open the Inline Dialog.

6

APEX PAGE DESIGNER

The Page Designer is one of the main features and a major improvement for APEX developers. It changes the way we build our application pages and the way we think about the development of our application.Page Designer is a full featured Integrated Development Environment (IDE) that includes a toolbar and multiple panes.

The Page Designer window features has three panes:

- Left pane
- Central pane
- Right pane

The Left pane includes four tabs: Rendering, Dynamic Actions, Processing and Page Shared Components.

The central pane contains four tabs: Layout, Component View, Page Search and Help.

The right pane contains the Property Editor. Use the Property Editor to edit attributes of the selected component.

6.1 PAGE DESIGNER TOOLBAR

The Page Designer toolbar is displayed at the top of the page and contains both buttons and menu options.

The Page Designer toolbar includes the following buttons and menu options.

6.1.1 Page Selector

The current page is displayed in the Page Selector. To search for pages, click the down arrow. Alternatively, enter the page number of the field and click Go.

6.1.2 Page Unlocked and Page Locked

Page Unlocked indicates that the current page is unlocked and editable. Page Locked indicates that the page is not available for editing.

6.1.3 Undo and Redo

Undo reverses the previous update / changes we made with the Page Designer. Redo updates the last update that has been undone using Undo.

6.1.4 Create

Features a graphic plus (+) sign. Create menu options to include:

MENU OPTION	MENU USAGE
Page	Access to a Page Create Wizard
Page as Copy	Access to the Copy Page Wizard

Page Component	Summary of how to create Page Components in Page Designer
Breadcrumb Region	Access to the Create Breadcrumb Wizard
Shared Component	Access to the Create Application Component Wizard. Shared components are common elements that can be displayed or used on any page of the application
Page Group	Links to the page of the Page Group. Use the page groups to organize your pages
Developer Comments	Access the Developer Comments dialog. Developers may add comments to an application, page or group of pages

6.1.5 Utilities

Features a graphic of a wrench. The menu options of the utilities include:

MENU OPTION	MENU USAGE
Delete Page	Delete your current page
Advisor	Access to Oracle APEX Advisor (Advisor). Use the Advisor to verify the integrity and quality of your Oracle APEX application
Caching	Links to the Caching page. Enable caching is an effective way to improve performance
Attribute Dictionary	Access the Attribute Dictionary
History	Displays a report of changes to the current page
Export	Export the current page
Cross Page Utilities	Access Cross Page Utilities
Application Utilities	Access Application Utilities
Page Groups	Links to the page of the Page Group. Use the page groups to organize your pages
Upgrade Application	Upgrade your existing application

6.1.6 Shared Components

Links to your Shared Components page. Shared components can be displayed or used on any page within the application.

6.1.7 Save and Run Page

Click Save to save your current page. Click Run Page to save and then run the current page.

6.2 LEFT PANE OF PAGE DESIGNER

The left pane of the Page Designer includes four tabs: Rendering, Dynamic Actions, Processing and Page Shared Components. Each tab shows a list of the corresponding component types and components created on the current page.

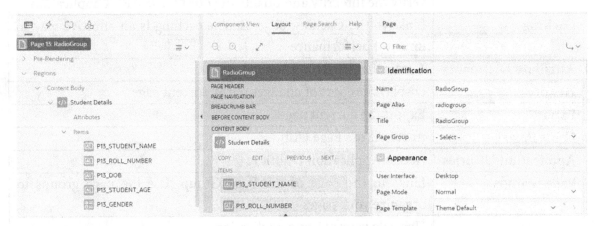

6.2.1 Rendering Tab

The Rendering tab will display regions, page items, page buttons, page components and application logic. The Rendering tab groups and orders components based on how they are processed by Oracle APEX.

6.2.3 Dynamic Actions Tab

The Dynamic Actions tab shows dynamic actions defined on the current page. By creating a dynamic action, you can declaratively define complex client-side behavior without the need for JavaScript.

6.2.4 Processing Tab

The Processing tab shows the application logic defined on the page and the groups and orders components based on how Oracle APEX processes them.

6.2.5 Page Shared Components Tab

The Page Shared Components tab shows the shared components associated with this page.

6.3 CENTRAL PANE OF PAGE DESIGNER

The central pane of the Page Designer contains four tabs: Layout, Component View, Page Search and Help. The following topics provide a detailed discussion of how to use these tabs when editing a page.

6.3.1 Layout Tab

The Layout tab shows how the components are positioned on the page in the central pane of the Page Designer. The context menus feature on the Layout tab. By selecting a component and right-clicking, you can delete, move or copy the component to other regions or to new regions on the page. You can move existing regions, items and buttons relative to other components by simply clicking the component and drag it to a new location.

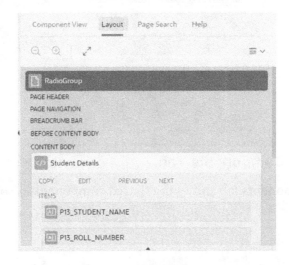

6.3.2 Component View Tab:

Similar to the App Builder Legacy Component View window, the Component View tab groups user interface elements and application logic by component type. The Component View tab is displayed in the central pane of the Page Designer and consists of the following sections:

Page rendering - Page rendering is a process that generates a page from a database. Use the page rendering section to modify controls that affect page rendering, including page attributes, regions, buttons, items, page rendering computations and page processes.

Page Processing - The Page Processing is the process of submitting the page. Typically, a page is submitted when the user clicks on a Button. Use the Page Processing section to specify application logic such as computations, validation, process and branching. In general, this logic is run by the APEX engine in the order it appears on the page.

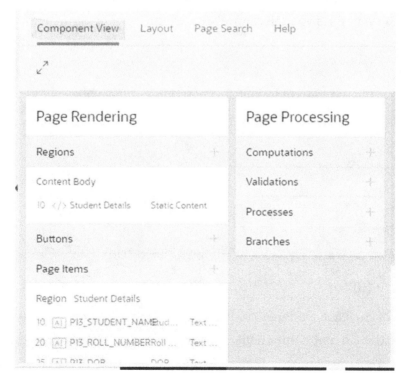

6.3.3 Page Search Tab

Use Page Search to search for all the metadata of the page, including regions, items, buttons, dynamic actions, columns and so on. To search a page, enter a search term in the field provided. Select Match Case to match the case. Select Regular Expression to search for a regular expression.

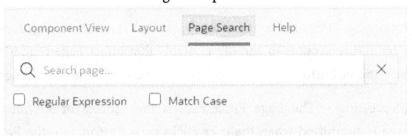

6.3.4 Help Tab

Page Designer includes Help for every attribute of the Property Editor. To see Help, select the attribute and click the Help tab. Once you activate the Help pane, the content that displays changes every time you select another attribute.

6.4 RIGHT PANE OF PAGE DESIGNER (PROPERTY EDITOR)

6.4.1 Property Editor

The right pane of the Page Designer contains the Property Editor. Property Editor displays all attributes of the current component. Clicking the View Component tab or the Search Page tab will also change the Editor Property selection. When selecting multiple components, the Property Editor will display only common attributes.Updating the common attribute updates the attribute for all the selected components.

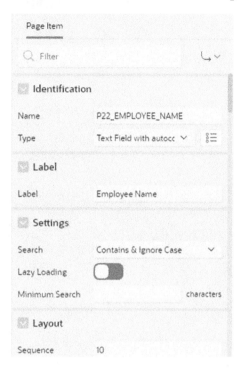

6.4.2 Code Editor

The Code Editor will be displayed as a modal dialog. We use the Code Editor to edit attributes that require a large amount of code. The Code Editor provides an enhanced code editor for editing the PL / SQL, SQL, HTML, CSS and JavaScript component properties.

SHARED COMPONENTS

7.1 APPLICATION LOGIC

The application Logic is one of the modules in Shared components, it consists of different types of features as listed below

- Application Definition Attributes
- Application Items
- Application Process
- Application Computations
- Application Settings
- Build options

7.1.1 Application Definition Attributes

This option helps the user to define basic characteristics of the application, including the application name, an optional alphanumeric alias and a version number.

In definition, regions or attributes values are also provided. Few of them are as follows

- Name
- Properties
- Application Icon
- Availability
- Error Handling
- Global Notification
- Substitutions

- Build Options

Name

This options helps the user to set the Application Name,Alias& Group.

Properties

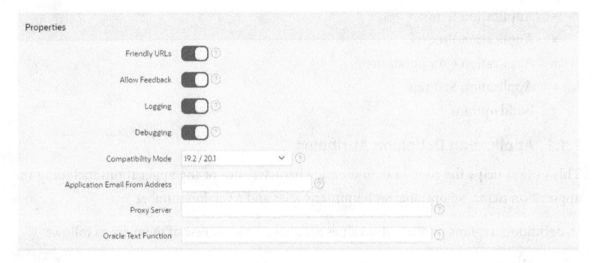

Application Icon

Availability

Error Handling

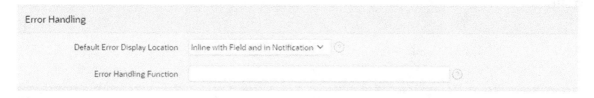

Global Notification

Substitutions

Build Options

7.1.2 Application Items

The User can use application Items to maintain session state. Application Items can be set using computations, processes or for passing values on a URL. Use "On New Instance" computations to set the value of items once for a session. Use Application Items to maintain session state that is not displayed and is not specific to any one page.

It consists of following attributes

Name

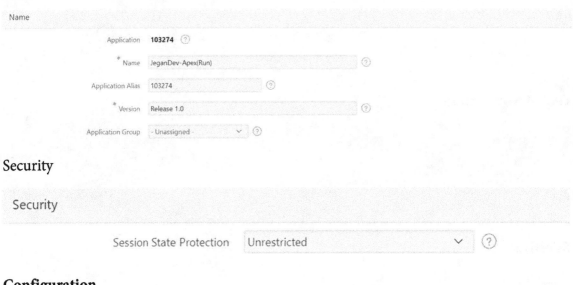

Security

Configuration

Comments

Comments

Comments

⑦

7.1.3 Application Process

Application Processes run PL/SQL logic at specific points for each page in an application or as defined by the conditions under which they are set to fire. Note that "Ajax Callback" processes fire only when called from Ajax or by "Run Ajax Callback" processes defined for pages. Few attributes are as follows

Name

Name

Application:	103274 JeganDev-Apex(Run) ⑦
* Sequence	1 ⑦
* Process Point	Ajax Callback: Run this application process when requested by a page process. ∨ ⑦
* Name	DOWNLOADPDF ⑦
Type	**PL/SQL Anonymous Block** ⑦

Source

Source

* PL/SQL Code ⑦

```
 1  begin
 2      for file in (select *
 3              from apex_application_temp_files
 4              where id = :FILE_ID) loop
 5
 6          sys.htp.init;
 7          sys.owa_util.mime_header( file.mime_type, FALSE );
 8          sys.htp.p('Content-length: ' || sys.dbms_lob.getlength( file.blob_content));
 9          sys.htp.p('Content-Disposition: attachment; filename="' || file.filename || '"' );
10          sys.htp.p('Cache-Control: max-age=3600');  -- tell the browser to cache for one hour, adjust as necessary
11          sys.owa_util.http_header_close;
12          sys.wpg_docload.download_file( file.blob_content );
13
14          apex_application.stop_apex_engine;
15      end loop;
16  end;
```

☐ Do not validate PL/SQL code (parse PL/SQL code at runtime only).

Conditions

Conditions

Condition Type   - Select Condition Type -   ⌄   ⑦

PL/SQL   item / column=value   item / column not null   item / column null   request=e1   exists   never   none

Authorization

Authorization

Authorization Scheme   Must Not Be Public User   ⌄   ⑦

Configuration

Configuration

Build Option   - No Build Option -   ⌄   ⑦

Comments

Comments

Comments

⑦

7.1.4 Application

7.1.4.1 Computations

The user can use Application Computations to assign values to application and page items. It consists of below types as

Item

Frequency

Computation

Authorization

Conditions

Configurations

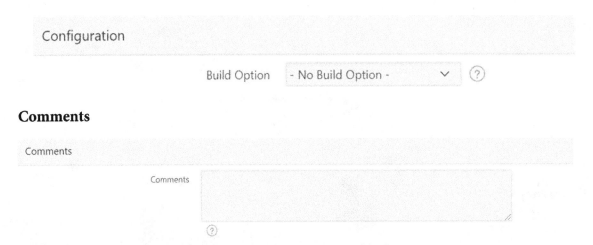

Comments

7.1.5 Application Settings

The Application Settings enable developers to define application level configuration options. You can use the following APIs within your application to access your application settings:

To set a value for a setting: apex_app_setting. set_value().

To get the value of a setting: apex_app_setting. get_value().

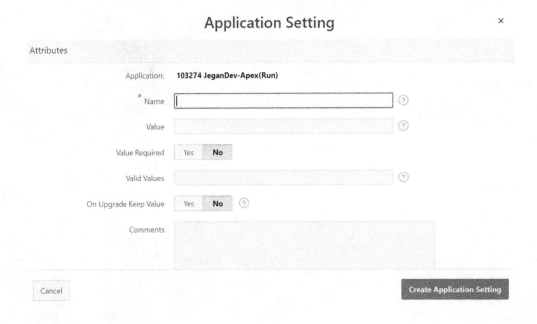

7.1.6 Build Options

The Build options enable developers to conditionally enable and disable application components and functionality when the application is installed or at run time using the GET_BUILD_OPTION_STATUS and SET_BUILD_OPTION_STATUS APIs.

The user can apply build options to most components (such as pages, regions, items, validations and so on) to include or exclude them in the run time application:

7.1.6.1   Creating Build Options

This option helps the user to create build options by selecting the application and accessing Build Options on the Shared Components page.

7.1.6.2   Including or Excluding Build Options

The user can specify Include to enable a component and include it with the application. Specify Exclude to disable a component and exclude it from the application.

7.1.6.3   Selecting a Build Option

This option helps the user can apply build options to a page, component, page control or shared component in Page Designer.

7.1.6.4   Deleting Build Options and Associated Components

It helps the user to delete a build option by first removing the associated components and then deleting the build option.

7.1.6.5   *Viewing Build Option Reports*

This option helps to access the Utilization report where build options are utilized in the current application. View the History report to see what modifications have been made to build options in the current application.

7.1.6.6   *Exporting Build Options or Build Option Status*

This option helps the user to export build option status to toggle build options on or off within another environment. It Consists of two types as below

Include: It defines that components are enabled and part of the application.

Exclude: It Defines that components are disabled and not part of the application.

7.2   SECURITY

The general question on security of browser-based APEX application is "How secured is your application?" The best answer for that question is "Oracle store is built with Oracle APEX ". It is one of the secured applications one could perform even financial transaction using APEX.

Configuring the attributes on the Edit Security Attributes page will protect your application. The protection attributes are grouped into the following categories:

- Security Attributes
- Authentication Schemes
- Authorization Schemes
- Application Access Control
- Session State Protection
- Web Credentials

7.2.1   Security Attributes

This option helps the user to use this page to set application-wide security settings. Edit application components directly to manage more granular settings.

It consists of some following features as below

7.2.1.1 Authentication

Authentication is the process of establishing each user's identify before they can access your application. You may define multiple authentication schemes for your application, however only one scheme can be current. The authentication logic of the current scheme is used when your application is run.

7.2.1.2 Authorization

Application authorization schemes control access to all pages within an application. Unauthorized access to the application, regardless of which page is requested, will cause an error page to be displayed.

7.2.1.3 Session Management

This option helps to control the application session management. Use attributes of Session Management to decrease the exposure to abandoned computers with an open web browser by the application. Session state management is done with the session ID and this session values will be maintained by the item in the browser and developer can restrict the values being changed by the users.

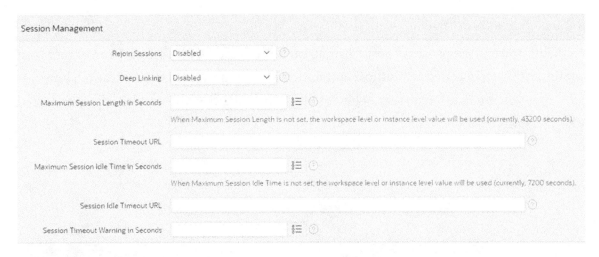

7.2.1.4 Session State Protection

Enabling Session State Protection can prevent hackers from tampering with URLs within your application. URL tampering can adversely affect program logic, session state contents and information privacy.

To enable Session State Protection for your application, select Enabled from the Session State Protection list. Enabling Session State Protection turns on session state protection controls defined at the page and item level. To configure Session State Protection, click Manage Session State Protection.

7.2.1.5 Browser Security

This option helps to control the application Browser Security Management.

7.2.1.6 Database Session

This option helps to control the application Database Session management.

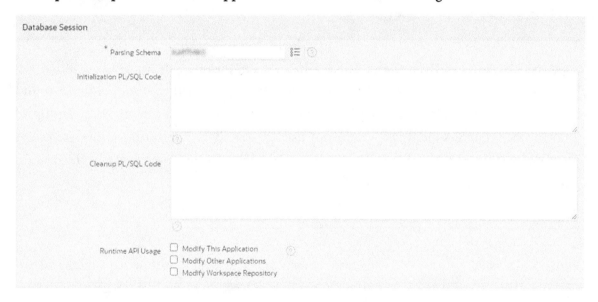

7.2.2 Authentication Schemes

Authentication is the method of defining the users before they can access an application. While multiple authentication schemes can be established for your application, only one scheme can be up to date at a time.

- **Application Express accounts** – this uses user accounts and passwords that are created and managed within Oracle APEX user repository. Your application is authenticated against these accounts.

- **Custom** – as always there will be different needs for different users hence this enables them to sculpture their own authentication using PLSQL program
- **Database account** – this uses the schema username and password from the database where APEX is installed this act more like no authentication
- **HTTP Header variable** – this is used only for the single sign on from some other application
- **LDAP directory** – when you have LDAP server you can use the same credentials maintained in the server
- **Oracle Server single sign on** -this uses the credentials maintained in oracle server

7.2.3 Authorization Schemes

Authorization schemes control access to all applications pages. An error page can be triggered by an unauthorized access to the application/page after configuring Authorization scheme. Many of the users still get puzzled with the authentication and authorization. The basic difference is the authentication is like a lock in your laptop of desktop which enables the user to login and use the system, but authorization is like access given for each user to use only software allowed to them. We can define the authorization at each item level also.

Authorization Scheme Types	Description
Exists SQL Query	Enter a query that causes the authorization scheme to pass if it returns at least one row and causes the scheme to fail if it returns no rows
NOT Exists SQL Query	Enter a query that causes the authorization scheme to pass if it returns no rows and causes the scheme to fail if it returns one or more rows
PL/SQL Function Returning Boolean	Enter a function body. If the function returns true, the authorization succeeds.

Authorization Scheme Types	Description
Item in Expression 1 is NULL	Enter an item name. If the item is null, the authorization succeeds.
Item in Expression1 is NOT NULL	Enter an item name. If the item is not null, the authorization succeeds.
Value of Item in Expression 1 Equals Expression 2	Enter and item name and value. The authorization succeeds if the item's value equals the authorization value.
Value of Item in Expression 1 Does NOT Equal Expression 2	Enter an item name and a value. The authorization succeeds if the item's value is not equal to the authorization value.
Value of Preference in Expression 1 Does NOT Equal Expression 2	Enter a preference name and a value. The authorization succeeds if the preference's value is not equal to the authorization value.
Value of Preference in Expression 1 Equals Expression 2	Enter a preference name and a value. The authorization succeeds if the preference's value equal the authorization value.
Is In Group	Enter a group name. The authorization succeeds if the group is enabled as a dynamic group for the session. See "APEX_AUTHORIZATION.ENABLE_DYNAMIC_GROUPS" in Oracle Application Express API Reference. If the application uses APEX Accounts Authentication, this check also includes workspace groups that are granted to the user. If the application uses Database Authentication, this check also includes database roles

Authorization Scheme Types	Description
	that are granted to the user.
Is Not In Group	Enter a group name. The authorization succeeds if the group is not enabled as a dynamic group for the session.

Source: https://docs.oracle.com/html/E39147_04/sec_authorization.htm

7.2.4 Application Access Controls

Access Control requires developers to define users and roles of the applications. Because roles are assigned to users, roles must be generated before the users are implemented. You may delegate one or more of the functions to users. You need to create an Authorization Scheme to control access to the application pages and components.

Roles and users defined for applications can be reviewed using the following views:

- APEX_APPL_ACL_USERS
- APEX_APPL_ACL_USER_ROLES
- APEX_APPL_ACL_ROLES

Source: https://docs.oracle.com/en/database/oracle/application-express/20.1/AEAPI/toc.htm

7.2.5 Session State Protection

Enabling session state protection within your application can prevent hackers from tampering with URLs. Tampering the URL can adversely affect program logic, content in the session state and privacy of information. Enable either the Edit Security Attributes page or the Session State Protection page to protect session State.

When Session State Security is passed, the next step is to configure the protection attributes. The protection attributes can be configured in two ways:

- Use a wizard and choose a value for categories of attributes. Those selections will then apply to all applicable pages and items.

- Set up values for individual pages, items or application items.

7.2.6 Web Credentials

Using Web Credentials to connect to REST Enabled SQL or any other external REST services. Application Express stores safely and encrypts these keys for use by the Application Express and API modules. Credentials can not be retrieved in a clear text.

Credentials are stored at the workspace level and are thus available in all applications. If you export a document, the used credential will be added to the export file.

When you migrate an application to another workspace, Application Express tests if the target workspace already contains the same static ID. If a credential already exists, it is used by the application. Otherwise, the import file credential will be generated in the target workspace.

Source:https://docs.oracle.com/en/database/oracle/application-express/20.1//htmdb/ managing-credentials.html#GUID-5409A100-3FEE-424A-AF45-07211F69A0BA

7.3 OTHER COMPONENTS

The following are the list of other components that are under shared components.

1. List of values
2. Plug-ins
3. Component settings
4. Shortcuts
5. Email Templates

We can see below about how to create the components and their details

7.3.1 List of Values

A list of values (LOV) is a static or dynamic set of values used to display a pop-up list of values, select list, check box or radio group.

In the following example we can create sample LOV with name as "Test" and place the SQL Query in Query box.

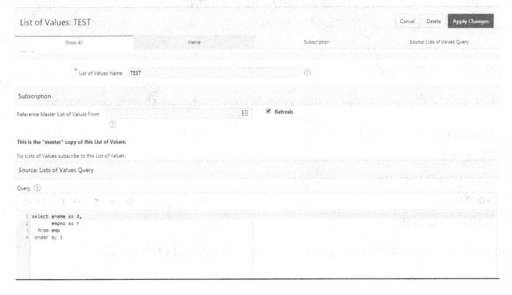

#Sample Code

```
select ename as d, empno as r
from emp
order by 1
```

We can include the shared component LOV on the Page level item creation. In List of Values, set the type as "*Shared Components*" and in List if values set as "Test".

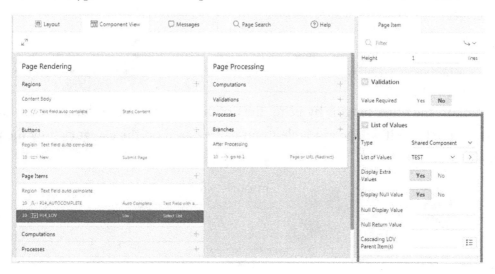

7.3.2 Plug-ins

App Builder includes built-in item types, region types, dynamic actions and processes. Use plug-ins to add new declarative types into your application.

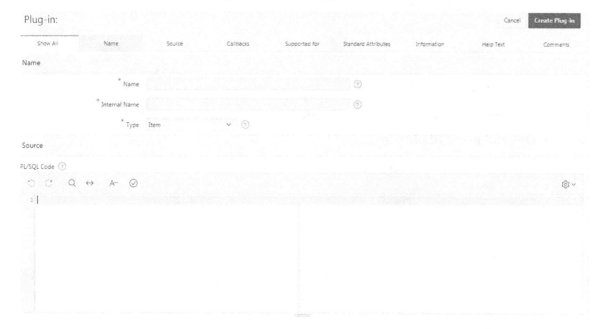

We can create a new plugin and assign the name for it.In PLSQL Code, we can set the process code for the plugin and that can be used in regions type,Item type, dynamic actions and processes

We can import the other plugins by using the option "Import" and it has been included as Application level and it will be available in all pages based on the category how the plugin has been created.

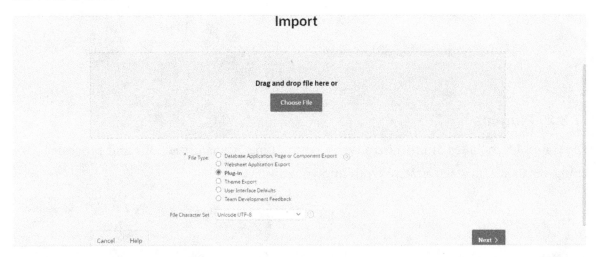

7.3.3 Component Settings

Use Component Settings to set application-level values for built-in Oracle APEX components and installed plug-ins.

7.3.4 Shortcuts

Use shortcuts to avoid repetitive coding of HTML or PL/SQL functions. You can create a shortcut to define a page control such as a button, HTML text, a PL/SQL procedure or HTML. Once you define a shortcut, it is stored in a central repository so you can reference it from various locations within your application.

Shortcuts are a repository of shared static or dynamic HTML. Shortcuts are substitution strings that are expanded using the syntax: "SHORTCUT_NAME". Shortcuts are used in the following locations:

1. Region Source for regions of type HTML_WITH_SHORTCUTS
2. Region Templates, Region Headers & Footers
3. Item Labels
4. Item Default Value
5. Item Post Element Text
6. Item Help Text
7. HTML Header of a page

7.3.5 Email Templates

Create templates to define the HTML format and Plain Text formats for the emails you wish to send from an application.

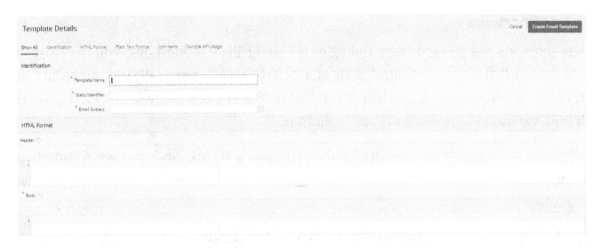

Before we send email from an application, your Instance administrator must log in to Oracle Application Express Administration Services, navigate to the Instance Settings page and configure Email attributes.

- Template Name - Enter a descriptive name for this template.
- Static Identifier - Static string identifier used to refer to the template when calling the APEX_MAIL APIs.
- Email Subject - Enter the text to display for the email subject.
- Define the Header, Body and Footer. Body supports basic HTML markup.
- Under Advanced, optionally click Load Default HTML.
- The default HTML appears in the HTML Template. If needed, edit the default HTML Template.
- Under Plain Text Format, enter the appropriate template defaults.
- Under Comments, optionally enter comments that describe this template.
- Click Create Email Template.
- Next, create a button and process to call the APEX_MAIL API to send email.

Source: https://docs.oracle.com/en/database/oracle/application-express/ 18.2/htmdb/shared-components-page.html#GUID-A3FBCD13-FF7A-45F0-8DCB-B45C18EFCAC7

7.4   NAVIGATION

Navigation is an important part of the application and determine how users can navigate within the application. The Navigation region on the shared component has the following links:

- Lists
- Navigation Menu
- Breadcrumbs
- Navigation Bar List

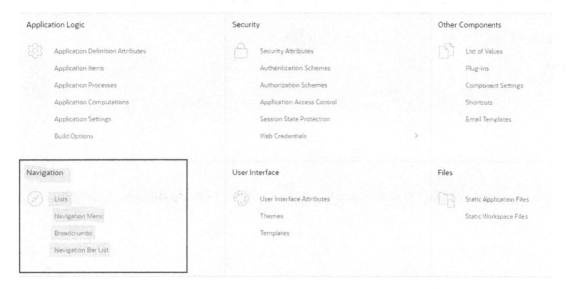

7.4.1 Lists

The collection of links is a list. A list will be available under Navigation region on the Shared Components. The appearance of the list display in the page is based on the list templates. Each list can be control by adding a display condition to it. Let's see how to create a list,

Two types of lists can be created,

- Static Lists
- Dynamic Lists

7.4.1.1 Static Lists

A Static List is based on predefined display and return values. When you wish to create a static list, a list entry label and a target (either a page or URL) attributes needs to be defined. A static list can be creating using the following option, creating from scratch, by copying existing entries or by adding the list entries. Each list will have display condition, which enables to control its display.

The following describes how to create a Static List,

Step 1: Navigate to the application shared components.

Step 2: Create the list using the Create List Wizard.

Step 3: Mention whether to create the list from scratch or by copying an existing list.

Step 4: If the option from scratch is chosen, then enter the details for the Name, select type as Static and click next.

Step 5: Define a list entry and click next.

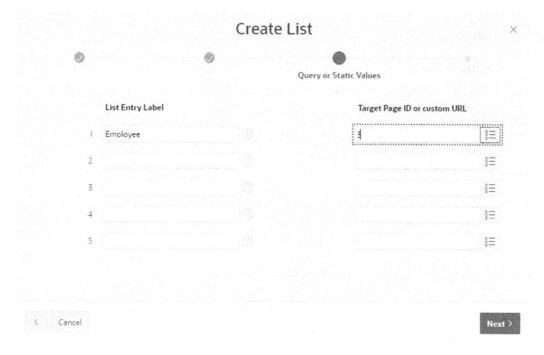

Step 6: Specify the details for Create List regions and click Create list.

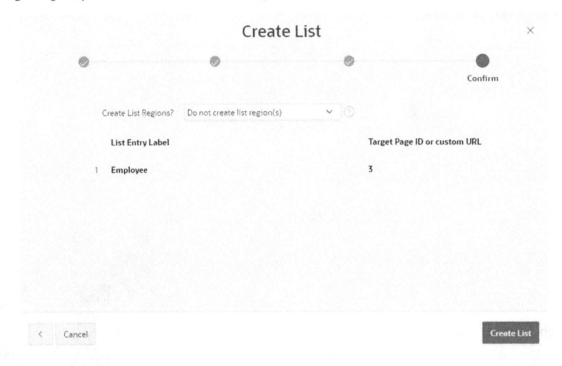

7.4.1.2 Dynamic List

A Dynamic list is based on a SQL query or a PL/SQL function executed at runtime. Using Dynamic list, a list can be created dynamically which will also support for mobile frameworks.

The list definition displays a specific type of page item, such as progress bars, sidebar, bullet navigation list or navigation menu. You can control how a list displays through templates.

The following describes the process to create Dynamic List,

Step 1: Navigate to the application shared components.

Step 2: Create the list by using the Create List Wizard.

Step 3: Mention whether to create the list from scratch or by copying an existing list.

Step 4: If the option "from scratch" is chosen, then enter the details for the Name , Select type as Dynamic and click next.

Step 5: Enter a SQL query or a PL/SQL function returning a SQL query.

Step 6: Add the list to a page by creating a List region.

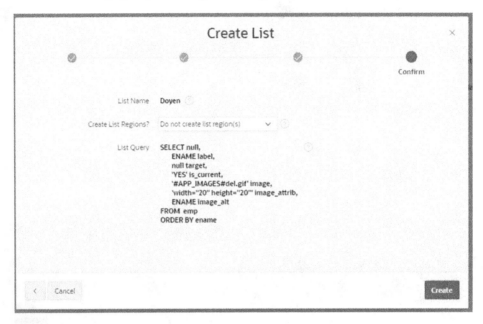

7.4.2 Navigation Menu

A navigation menu is a list links that enables users to navigate the pages in an application. Navigation menus are only supported in the applications using the Universal Theme.

The primary navigation structure for your application is defined as a Navigation Menu and is based on the List component in APEX. Navigation Menus are hierarchical and can be any level deep. This navigation control and can be both dynamic (based on a query) or static (based on static list entries).

Click "Desktop Navigation Menu" and it will redirect to the list of entries under the Desktop Navigation Menu and Click "Create Entry" to create a list entry .

The example below shows with a navigation menu displaying as a sidebar. In this example, the navigation menu includes list entries for the application pages: Home; Student Master; Calender; Map Chart etc.

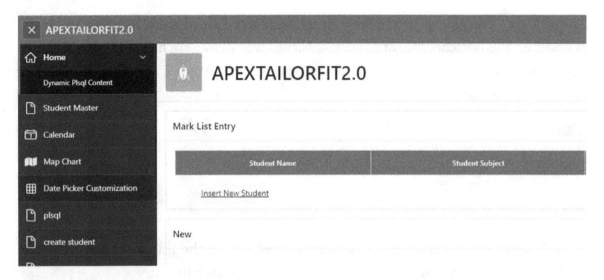

7.4.3 Breadcrumbs

A breadcrumb is a hierarchical list of links that shows where the user is within the application from a hierarchical perspective. It helps the users to click a specific breadcrumb link to view the page instantly. We can use breadcrumbs as a second level of navigation which will always place at the top of the page, complementing other user interface elements such as tabs and lists.

Below are the steps to create a breadcrumb and assign it to the page Breadcrumb region.

Step 1: Click "Create Breadcrumb" and enter the breadcrumb name as "Breadcrumbdev" and click Create.

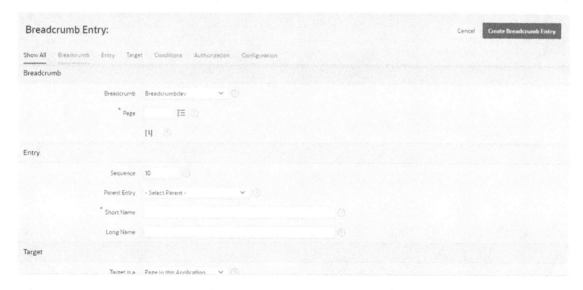

Step 2: Select "Breadcrumbdev" and Click "Create Breadcrumb Entry" and enter a short name as "Home" and assign a page as 1.

Step 3: create breadcrumb Entries for Employee Creation and Employee Address Details.

- For "Employee Creation", set the Parent Entry as "Home".
- For "Employee Address Details", set the Parent Entry as "Employee Creation".

The below image shows that the newly created breadcrumb has been assigned to page breadcrumb region and it will the display the list of hierarchical links.

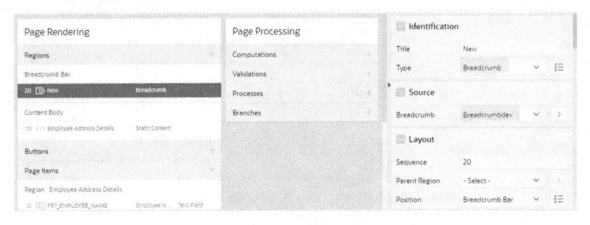

7.4.4 Navigation Bar List

The Navigation Bar is positioned near the end of the application's header and typically contains links for user authentication, help, feedback and other global items.Navigation bar lists enable users to create a simple navigation path for migrating between pages in an application. The section of a navigation bar depends upon the associated page template. A list entry can be an image, an image with text beneath it or text.

Click "Navigation Bar List" and select the Desktop Navigation Bar.

Under the Desktop navigation Bar, Click "Create Entry" to create a list of entry .Eg. Sign Out.

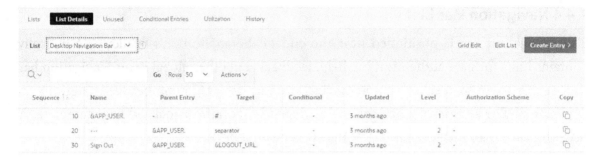

The example below shows with a navigation bar displaying at a application page header. In this example, the navigation bar includes list entry for "Sign out" and it helps users to logout from the application.

7.5 USER INTERFACE

The user interface consists of three major module as mentioned below, which is used to define various key parameters and attributes of the application.

- User Interface Attributes
- Themes
- Templates

7.5.1 User Interface Attributes

On the Shared Component page, edit User Interface attributes under the User Interface section to determine the application's default characteristics and optimize the display for the target environment (such as Desktop or Mobile).

Attributes enable you to select the home and login pages that users are redirected to when they access this user interface. You can also set the current theme style and global page.

Using the Navigation Menu, you can select the list and position used to render the navigation menu as well as setting the navigation menu list template.

Navigation Bar settings enable you to select list and list templates. Selecting classic implementation uses tabs instead of a list.

The JavaScript, Cascading Style Sheet and Concatenated Files attributes can be used to select alternate content delivery networks, load additional CSS files and to optimize the way JavaScript and CSS files are loaded.

7.5.2 Theme

Themes are sets of templates enabling developers to determine the structure and design of an application. Themes provide developers with a full set of templates that can fit any UI pattern that an application can require. Templates are first grouped by type of template and then by the class of template. Types of templates include page, region, report, list, button, label and LOV.

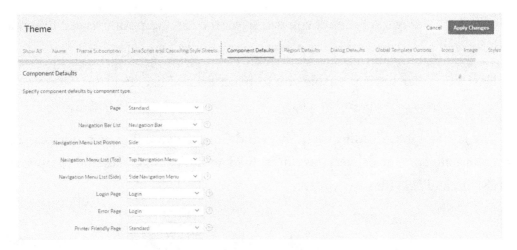

There are several template classes for each template type. In a template type, a template class determines the function of a template. For example, a template for a region may be categorized as a template for a type region, a template for a report region, etc.

Universal Theme-42 (Common Theme) helps developers to create modern web applications without the need for comprehensive HTML, CSS or JavaScript expertise. For your APEX applications, Universal Theme is a responsive, flexible and customizable user interface.

There are several options for editing the theme using the methods below,

- Copy theme
- Delete theme
- Import theme
- Export theme

7.5.2.1 Copy theme

Theme installed in the APEX application can be copied by selecting the copy theme button.

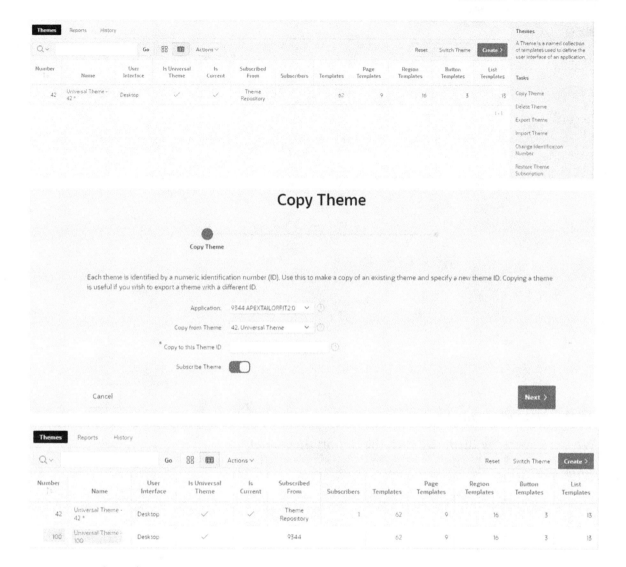

7.5.2.2 Delete Theme:

Delete the theme by clicking the button "Delete Theme" and click Next and finally click Delete Theme button to delete the theme.

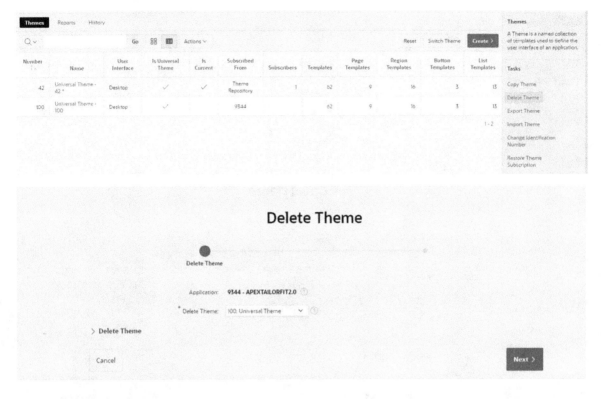

7.5.2.3   Import Theme

We can import the theme by click the Import theme button.

7.5.2.4 Export theme

We can Export the theme by click the Export theme button.

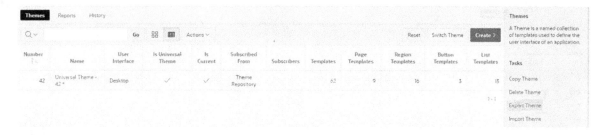

7.5.2.5 Switch Theme

Switch theme option is used to switch the old theme to new theme.

7.5.3 Template

The APEX engine generates a user interface based on a series of named collection of templates called a theme. Templates in an application monitor the look and feel of the components. When you must build a custom design, starting with an existing template is usually more straightforward. You can create one or more default templates to change the style of the templates to match your unique needs.

To edit template attributes, select the template name. To preview a template, click the Run icon.

In the below we can change the button template.

Button templates enable developers to customize the look and feel of a button. To build a button, you can use multiple images or HTML tags. Using button templates is optional.

To edit the template, we can copy the template and set the new name for the template and then we can edit based on the what we need.

The below are the template types for the buttons like Normal Template and Hot Template.

We can change the HTML to edit the buttons look and feel. Once we created the new template then it will be reflected on all the pages.

If we want to change the button look based on what we customize then we can select the newly created template name for the button.

Source:https://docs.oracle.com/en/database/oracle/application-express/18.2/htmdb/shared-components-page.html#GUID-A3FBCD13-FF7A-45F0-8DCB-B45C18EFCAC7

7.6 FILES

The File region on the shared component has the following links,

- Static Application Files
- Static Workspace Files

7.6.1 Static Application Files

Static application files are only available to the current application. Use #APP_IMAGES# in your application to reference a file.

The Static Application Files link enables you to upload, view, download and delete the files which include images, CSS files, js files and other files. This can be managed within application level.

To practice the above-mentioned action, follow the steps given below,

To Upload,

Step 1: Navigate to the shared component page in application.

Step 2: Select Static Application files under Files.

Step 3: Click Upload to upload file.

Step 4: Enter the name of the directory in the directory field where the file should be stored.
Step 5: If nothing is specified then by default the file will be stored in the root directory.

Step 6: Select file to be uploaded by specifying in File.

Step 7: Mention the character set encoding for the file if required.

Step 8: Select the option Yes/No for unzip file.

Step 9: Click Upload.

To View and Delete,

Step 1: Navigate to the shared component page in application.

Step 2: Select Static Application files under Files.

Step 3: A Report appears. A Column File Name will act as link to edit the files.

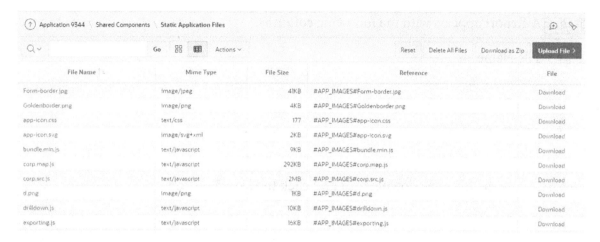

Step 4: Click any of the filename.

Step 5: Information will be displayed in the pop up as below.

Step 6: To delete, click Delete button.

Step 7: To exit, click Exit button.

To Download,

Step 1: Navigate to the shared component page in application.

Step 2: Select Static Application files under Files.

Step 3: A Report appears with the following columns,

- File Name
- Mime Type
- File Size
- Reference
- File

Step 4: Locate the file to be downloaded and click the Download link.

File Name	Mime Type	File Size	Reference	File
Form-border.jpg	image/jpeg	41KB	#APP_IMAGES#Form-border.jpg	Download
Goldenborder.png	image/png	4KB	#APP_IMAGES#Goldenborder.png	Download
app-icon.css	text/css	177	#APP_IMAGES#app-icon.css	Download
app-icon.svg	image/svg+xml	2KB	#APP_IMAGES#app-icon.svg	Download
bundle.min.js	text/javascript	9KB	#APP_IMAGES#bundle.min.js	Download
corp.map.js	text/javascript	292KB	#APP_IMAGES#corp.map.js	Download
corp.src.js	text/javascript	2MB	#APP_IMAGES#corp.src.js	Download
d.png	image/png	1KB	#APP_IMAGES#d.png	Download
drilldown.js	text/javascript	10KB	#APP_IMAGES#drilldown.js	Download

7.6.2 Static Workspace Files

Static workspace files are available to all applications for a given workspace. Use #WORKSPACE_IMAGES# in your application to reference a file.

The Static Workspace Files link enables you to upload, view, download and delete the files which include images, CSS files, js files and other files. This can be managed by workspace level.

To practice the above-mentioned action, follow the steps given below,

To Upload,

Step 1:Navigate to the shared component page in application.

Step 2:Select Static Workspace files under Files.

Step 3:Click Upload to upload file.

Step 4: Enter the name of the directory in the directory field where the file should be stored. If nothing is specified, then by default the file will be stored in the root directory.

Step 5: Select file to be uploaded by specifying in File.

Step 6: Mention the character set encoding for the file if required.

Step 7: Select the option Yes/No for unzip file.

Step 8: Click Upload.

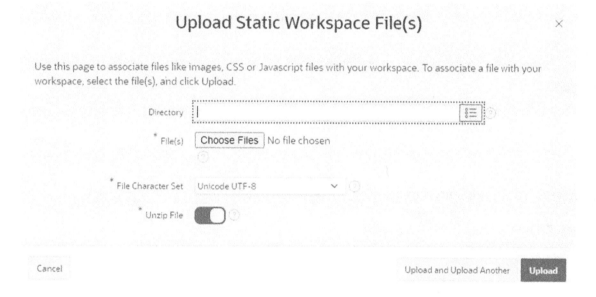

To View and Delete,

Step 1: Navigate to the shared component page in application.

Step 2: Select Static Workspace files under Files.

Step 3:A Report appears. A Column File Name will act as link to edit the files.

Step 4:Click any of the filename.

Step 5:Information will be displayed in the pop up.

Edit Static Workspace File ☒

File Name: **Doyensys log.png** ⑦

Mime Type: **image/png** ⑦

Image:

DOYENSYS
Technology Drives, We Lead

Cancel   Delete

Step 6:Click Delete button to delete.

Step 7:To exit, click Exit button.

To Download,

Step 1:Navigate to the shared component page in application.

Step 2:Select Static Workspace files under Files.

Step 3:A Report appears with the following columns,

- File Name
- Mime Type
- File Size
- Reference
- File

Step 4:Locate the file to be downloaded and click the Download link.

7.7 REPORTS

The Reports is one of the components in Shared Components and it consists of below two types.

- Report Queries
- Report layouts

7.7.1 Report Queries

Defining a report query on the shared component helps to print report region within the current application. A report Queries identifies the info to be extracted. In contrast to SQL statements contained in regions, report queries contain SQL statements will be validated when the query is saved.

Note : Report queries should be SQL statements, not functions returning SQL statements.

Using "Output Format" option, we can match a report query and download it as a formatted document in the format we have defined. A generic layout is used if no report layout is selected. The purpose of the generic layout is to test and verify a report query. Only the first result set is included in the print document when using the generic layout option...

We can incorporate these reports with the application to make them accessible to end users. For example, a report query can be associated with a button, list item, branch or other navigation component that allows you to use URLs as targets. Then selecting that item starts the processing and downloading the report.

Creating a Report Layout

Step 1: Navigate to the shared component of your current application.

Step 2: Click Report Queries under Reports.

Step 3: Click Create.

Create Report Query   ×

Report Query Definition

Specify a name for your report query and select the output format. When using Oracle BI Publisher as the print server, you have a choice of exporting your report to PDF, Microsoft Word, Microsoft Excel and HTML. You can also allow the user to choose the output format at runtime using a page item to set the format. The name of the report query will be part of the request string in the URL used to download the report query. You can include session state of your current application in your report. Select this when you want to show additional data with your report. For example, you might want to include order header information along with order details in an order form.

* Report Query Name	
Output Format	PDF
Item	
View File As	Attachment
Session State	☐ Include application and session information

Cancel   Next >

Step 4: Specify the information for the following, then Click Next

- Report Query Name
- Output Format
- Item
- View file as
- Session State

Step 5: Provide the SQL statement for SQL query section.

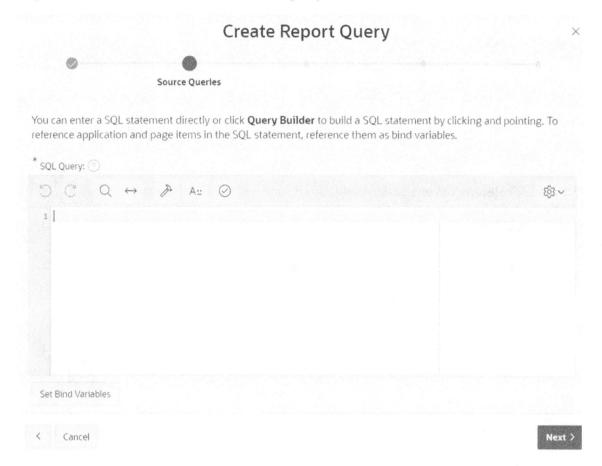

Step 6: Specify the information to Data Source for Report layout under Download Definition and Click Next.

Step 7: Provide the information for following, then Click Next

- Report Layout Source – If 'Create file based report layout' is selected then 'Report layout file' field is mandatory.
- Layout Name – Enter a layout name.
- Report Layout File – Click Browse and select Rich Text Editor.

Step 8: Final screen will be appear, view the information shown in the screen and click Create to create Report Query.

7.7.2 Report Layout

Using Report Layout, either a classic report region or a report query can be formatted and renders the data in a printer-friendly format. If a report layout is not selected, a default XSL-FO layout will be used. The default layout of XSL-FO is always used to make interactive reports region. Follow the below steps

To create a report layout

Step 1: Navigate to the shared components page.

Step 2: Click **Report Layout** under Reports.

Step 3: Click Create.

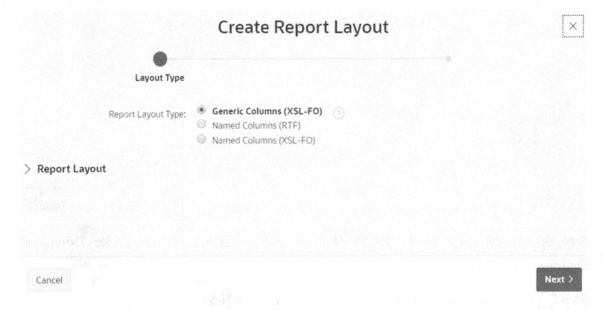

Step 4: Select a report layout type and click next.

- Generic Columns (XSL-FO) - Uses the default template to populate the report. You can customize the default code in the next step.
- Named Columns (XSL-FO) – If Named Columns (XSL-FO) is slected then it requires XSL-FO or RTF file to be upload in the next step.

Create Report Layout   ✕

⊘ ── ⬤

                                                    Layout Source

* Report Layout Name   [   ] ⊘

* Report Layout:
```
<?xml version = '1.0' encoding = 'utf-8'?>
<xsl:stylesheet version="2.0" xmlns:xsl="http://www.w3.org/1999/XSL/Transform"
xmlns:fo="http://www.w3.org/1999/XSL/Format"
xmlns:xlink="http://www.w3.org/1999/xlink">
    <xsl:variable name="_XDOFOPOS" select="''"/>
    <xsl:variable name="_XDOFOPOS2" select="number(1)"/>
    <xsl:variable name="_XDOFOTOTAL" select="number(1)"/>
    <xsl:variable name="_XDOFOOSTOTAL" select="number(0)"/>
```
⊘

* Report Column Heading:
```
                        <fo:table-cell xsl:use-attribute-sets="cell header-
color border">
                                <fo:block xsl:use-attribute-sets="text
#TEXT ALIGN#">
```
⊘

* Report Column:
```
                        <fo:table-cell xsl:use-attribute-sets="cell
border">
                                <fo:block xsl:use-attribute-sets="text
#TEXT ALIGN#">
```
⊘

* Report Column Width:
```
                    <fo:table-column column-width="#COLUMN_WIDTH#pt"/>
```
⊘

❮ Cancel   **Create Layout**

Step 5: Provide the appropriate information for the option shown. Note the option on this page will appears based on the report layout selection done in the previous page.

Step 6: Click Create Layout.

To Edit a report layout

Step 1: Navigate to the Shared Components page.

Step 2: Click Report layout under Report region.

Step 3: The report will be appeared with information if the report layout is created already.

Step 4: Select the layout want to edit.

Step 5: A pop up will appear, do the necessary changes and click Apply Changes. This is for generic column layouts.

Step 6: For named column layouts, click Download and do the changes in the file and upload the revised file.

Source:https://docs.oracle.com/en/database/oracle/application-express/19.1/htmdb/shared-components-page.html#GUID-C075D396-A6F6-4B1D-835A-58EC4240FFF8

7.8   GLOBALIZATION

The following are list of types under Globalization on the Shared Components page.

- Globalization Attributes
- Text Messages
- Translate Application

7.8.1 Globalization Attributes

We can develop applications that can run concurrently in different languages. Click this link to specify globalization options such as the Application Primary Language and Application Language Derived From attributes.

We can set the application date format once the date format has been set then it will be set for the whole application. Whenever we select the date from date picker it will set as the format that we mentioned in globalization.

7.8.1.1 Document Direction

We can set the document reading direction. By default, it's from left to right.We can also change from right to left.The below is the simple example to change the primary language type to "Chinese"

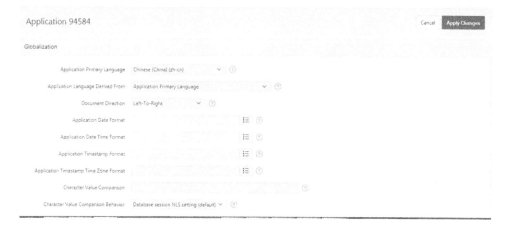

7.8.1.2 *Application Date format*

Once the Application date format has been set then it will be followed for whole application.By default, the date format is "DD-MON-RR", Now we are changing the format to "DD-MON-YYYY".

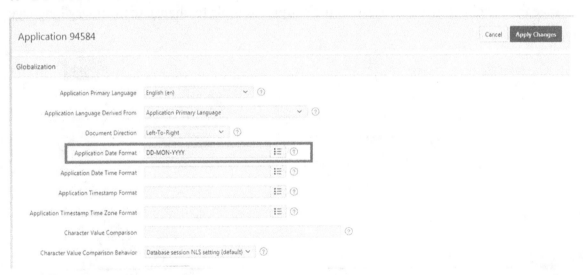

Now create a new date picker item and the format looks as below with format "DD-MON-YYYY". Once we create a new application then if set the format as above it will helps to reflect for all the pages.

Date
29-Sep-2019

7.8.2 Text Messages

Text Messages can be used to build translatable text strings with substitution variables that can be called from PL/SQL packages, procedures and functions.

We may need to translate messages if your application:

- Includes PL/SQL regions or PL/SQL processes or calls a PL/SQL package, procedure or function. If it does, you may need to translate the generated HTML.
- Uses a language that is not one of the ten languages into which Oracle APEX is translated. If it does, you may need to translate messages used in reports.

We can create text message by click the button "Create Text Message".

We create a new text message for the translation and set the name for it.

7.8.3 Translate Application

Applications can be translated from a primary language into other languages. Each translation results in the creation of a new translated application. Each translation requires a mapping which identifies the target language as well as the translated application ID. Translated applications cannot be edited directly in the App Builder.

Once the translation mappings are established the translatable text within the application is seeded into a translation repository. This repository can then be exported to an XLIFF for translation.

Once the XLIFF file is populated with the translations, one file per language, the XLIFF file is uploaded back into the translation repository. The final step is to publish each translated application from the translation repository.

A translated application will require synchronization when the primary application has been modified since the translated version was last published. Even modifications to application logic will require synchronization. To synchronize, seed and publish the translated application.

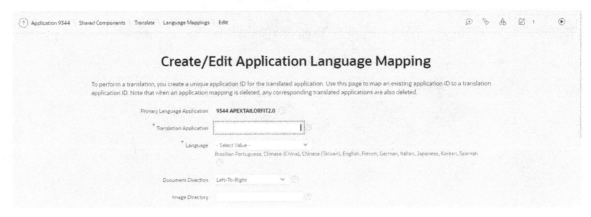

Click "Create", to create a new translated application.

Source:

https://docs.oracle.com/en/database/oracle/application-express/18.2/htmdb/translating-messages.html#GUID-2B07BBBC-AFF6-493D-B173-81C7C97C26DB

https://docs.oracle.com/en/database/oracle/application-express/18.2/htmdb/shared-components-page.html#GUID-270EA688-3883-4D37-8435-914648A25021

INTEGRATION WITH ANOTHER DATABASE WITHOUT DB LINK

When we say integration with another database. The first idea that comes to your mind is DB link. This was the scenario before web service. Now we can integrate two or more database to Oracle APEX without DB link. Let's see how to achieve it.

Web services is a standardized medium to transfer or transmit data between the client and server applications.

There are mainly two types of web services.

- SOAP web services.
- RESTful web services.

8.1 SOAP WEB SERVICE

SOAP Stands for Simple Object Access Protocol. This is an XML-based protocol for accessing web services.

SOAP is a recommendation of the W3C for communication between two applications.

SOAP is a protocol based on XML. The platform is independent and the language is independent. You will be able to interact with other programming language applications by using SOAP.

8.2   RESTFUL WEB SERVICES

REST stands for REpresentational State Transfer. REST is an architectural style not a protocol.

- It is fast because there is no strict specification such as SOAP. It consumes less bandwidth and more resources.

- It can be written in any programming language and executed on any platform.

- It can use SOAP web services as an implementation.

- It allows for different data formats, such as plain text, HTML, XML and JSON.

  The below are the methods that are used in RESTful web service

  1. **POST** – This would be used to create a new record using the RESTful web service
  2. **GET** - This would be used to get a list of all records using the RESTful web service
  3. **PUT** - This would be used to update all records using the RESTful web service
  4. **DELETE** - This would be used to delete all records using the RESTful web service

8.2.1   Steps to create endpoint

Step 1: From the Oracle APEX Home page, select the SQL Workshop tab and select the RESTful services.

Step 2: From RESTful services page, click "Create Module" Button.

Step 3:Under Oracle REST Data Services(**ORDS**) Module Definition Enter the Module Name, Base Path and other required details. Then click the "Create Module" Button.

Module Name: Book

Base Path: Doyensys

Step 4:After the has been Module Created, then click the "Create Template" Button.

Step 5: Under ORDS Template Definition Enter the URI template, Priority and HTTP Entity tag type.Then select the Create template option.

URI Template: Details

Priority: 0

HTTP Entity tag type: Secure Hash

*Step 6:*After Template created,Enter the below details in the Handler Page.

Method: Get

Source Type: SQL

Format: JSON

In "Source Editor"includethe below code and click the "Create Handler" Button.

Select * from emp

Step 7:Once the handler has been created, select the template name created by you and copy URL from full URL section. The below is the URL created from above steps.

https://apex.oracle.com/pls/apex/apextailorfit/Doyensys/Details

{"items":[{"empno":7839,"ename":"KING","job":"PRESIDENT","mgr":null,"hiredate":"1981-11-17T00:00:00Z","sal":5000,"comm":null,"deptno":10},
{"empno":7698,"ename":"BLAKE","job":"MANAGER","mgr":7839,"hiredate":"1981-05-01T00:00:00Z","sal":2850,"comm":null,"deptno":30},
{"empno":7782,"ename":"CLARK","job":"MANAGER","mgr":7839,"hiredate":"1981-06-09T00:00:00Z","sal":2450,"comm":null,"deptno":10},
{"empno":7566,"ename":"JONES","job":"MANAGER","mgr":7839,"hiredate":"1981-04-02T00:00:00Z","sal":2975,"comm":null,"deptno":20},
{"empno":7788,"ename":"SCOTT","job":"ANALYST","mgr":7566,"hiredate":"1982-12-09T00:00:00Z","sal":3000,"comm":null,"deptno":20},
{"empno":7902,"ename":"FORD","job":"ANALYST","mgr":7566,"hiredate":"1981-12-03T00:00:00Z","sal":3000,"comm":null,"deptno":20},
{"empno":7369,"ename":"SMITH","job":"CLERK","mgr":7902,"hiredate":"1980-12-17T00:00:00Z","sal":800,"comm":null,"deptno":20},
{"empno":7499,"ename":"ALLEN","job":"SALESMAN","mgr":7698,"hiredate":"1981-02-20T00:00:00Z","sal":1600,"comm":300,"deptno":30},
{"empno":7521,"ename":"WARD","job":"SALESMAN","mgr":7698,"hiredate":"1981-02-22T00:00:00Z","sal":1250,"comm":500,"deptno":30},
{"empno":7654,"ename":"MARTIN","job":"SALESMAN","mgr":7698,"hiredate":"1981-09-28T00:00:00Z","sal":1250,"comm":1400,"deptno":30},
{"empno":7844,"ename":"TURNER","job":"SALESMAN","mgr":7698,"hiredate":"1981-09-08T00:00:00Z","sal":1500,"comm":0,"deptno":30},
{"empno":7876,"ename":"ADAMS","job":"CLERK","mgr":7788,"hiredate":"1983-01-12T00:00:00Z","sal":1100,"comm":null,"deptno":20},
{"empno":7900,"ename":"JAMES","job":"CLERK","mgr":7698,"hiredate":"1981-12-03T00:00:00Z","sal":950,"comm":null,"deptno":30},
{"empno":7934,"ename":"MILLER","job":"CLERK","mgr":7782,"hiredate":"1982-01-23T00:00:00Z","sal":1300,"comm":null,"deptno":10}],"first":
{"$ref":"https://apex.oracle.com/pls/apex/apextailorfit/Doyensys/Details"}}

CONCLUSION

APEX is a mature, reliable, stable and indeed practical web development framework.

APEX helps to leverage the existing investment. It is a no cost tool forweb applications development on all Editions of the Oracle Database (Oracle Cloud, on-premises). It also enables to use advanced analytical queries, database level securitywithout any coding. APEX can be deployed with no cost middleware components like Tomcat and Glassfish. Short development duration than the alternatives in turn leads to lower cost and earlier deployment.

APEX eliminates the complexity of developing and deploying applications at all layers. The result is a low-code platform that is simpler, faster, lighter-weightthan the alternatives.The powerful components of APEX enable you to add a high-level of functionality to your apps with limited coding. We have also explored in this book the customizations with minimal coding, that will enhance further the functionalities of APEX Applications.

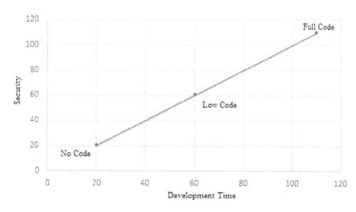

APEX has been designed from the very beginning to help developers build modern, beautiful, responsive applications without the need to become specialized experts. APEX applications can be developed by any developer with experience in SQL, PLSQL for server-side and HTML, CSS, JavaScript for the client-side.

Oracle APEX becomes a perfect RAD web application development tool for

- Developing new tailored applications
- Building Dashboards, Interactive and static Analytics or reports
- Integrating or Extending Oracle E-Business Suite with new functionality (on-premise & SaaS)

Oracle APEX has been widely used by various organizations to meet their medium to complex levels of application / website requirements. Please refer to the below URL for more details on the user success stories and different types of applications developed using Oracle APEX.

https://apex.world/ords/f?p=100:400:::NO:::

www.ingramcontent.com/pod-product-compliance
Lightning Source LLC
Chambersburg PA
CBHW080627060326
40690CB00021B/4838